Alan Billings has been a parish prie[s]
Kendal and has taught religious stud
Ripon College, Oxford and Queens C[o]
Deputy Leader of Sheffield City Council when David Blunkett was
Leader. He served on the Community Cohesion Panel of the Home
Office following the summer disturbances in 2001. He is a member
of the Youth Justice Board for England and Wales and the England
Committee of the Big Lottery Fund, and a regular contributor to BBC
Radio 4's 'Thought for the Day'. He is also the author of *Secular Lives
Sacred Hearts: The Role of the Church in a Time of No Religion* and
Dying and Grieving: A Guide to Pastoral Ministry.

GOD AND COMMUNITY COHESION

Help or hindrance?

Alan Billings

First published in Great Britain in 2009

Society for Promoting Christian Knowledge
36 Causton Street
London SW1P 4ST

The publisher and author acknowledge with thanks permission to
reproduce extracts from the following:

Extracts from The Book of Common Prayer, the rights in which are
vested in the Crown, are reproduced by permission of the Crown's
Patentee, Cambridge University Press

The Holy Qur'an, translated by Abdullah Yusuf Ali
(Ware: Wordsworth Editions, 2000).
Translation copyright © Islamic Vision, Birmingham

Every effort has been made to acknowledge fully the sources of material
reproduced in this book. The publisher apologizes for any omissions that
may remain and, if notified, will ensure that full acknowledgements are
made in a subsequent edition.

British Library Cataloguing-in-Publication Data
A catalogue record for this book is available from the British Library

ISBN 978–0–281–06084–9

1 3 5 7 9 10 8 6 4 2

Typeset by Graphicraft Limited, Hong Kong
Printed in Great Britain by Ashford Colour Press

Produced on paper from sustainable forests

I would like to dedicate the book to the next generation: my children and stepchildren and their partners – Hugh and Jennie, Guy and Hannah, Ruth and Colin, Alex and Debbie – and to Mantas Kazulis and Syeda Mehrin, students at Sheffield University, as they begin their life's work

Contents

Contents

Foreword

Following the launch of the Interfaith Foundation by Tony Blair in New York at the end of May 2008, this book is both timely and thought-provoking. Alan Billings has never ducked controversy, nor failed to take on the very big issues of the day. He does not let the reader down in this book.

At a time when there is much debate about the breakdown of family, of functioning communities and the disappearance of the glue that holds society together, it is important to take up and address many of the issues that currently face modern urban society. In the light of the changed attitude towards religion that sees a diminution in the traditional role of the Christian Church and a concomitant suspicion of the contribution Islam might make to cohesion and mutuality, it is valuable to examine how the public face of religions can be a positive rather than a negative feature. How does religious commitment contribute to rebuilding the role of civil society, and how can interfaith work overcome the polar impact of strong separate faiths meeting the needs of separate adherents within a common community? Alan Billings rightly recognizes that there is a fear of change. Not just suspicion, but a feeling that someone else is taking away the certainties on which life is based and, *in extremis*, that this poses a threat that for some evokes a negative reaction or even antagonism.

How can social cohesion be forged in this very different melting pot – with rapid global economic, social, cultural and spiritual change – and can faith be a help rather than a hindrance? These are the questions addressed in this thought-provoking and incisively written contribution to this vital debate.

I hope it will be widely read and discussed, but above all that it will have an impact on those responsible for policy and those engaged in positive action on the ground. For if the glue of the past is to be replaced by the adhesive of the future, then all of us have an interest in making pluralism a force for good rather than fragmentation, suspicion and division; a force for evil.

David Blunkett MP

Acknowledgements

I am grateful to a number of people for conversations I have had with them over many years around the various themes in this book. There have been friends and colleagues at Lancaster University, especially Dr Andrew Holden and Professors Ian Reader and Paul Heelas; at St George's Church, Kendal, especially my curates, the Revds Chris Taylor, Jean Radley and Beverley Lock, and my churchwardens, Val Carradus and Arnold Brockbank; at the Youth Justice Board for England and Wales; and at the Big Lottery Fund. There have also been friends of long standing from whose wisdom I have benefited, especially David Blunkett MP, Clive Betts MP, David Skinner and Pat Coleman in Sheffield; and, more recently, Simon Henderson at the Washington Institute and Dina Gold from the Board of Deputies of Jews. Needless to say, they are not directly responsible for the views I express; but I thank them all.

The research Dr Andrew Holden and I undertook in Burnley in 2006–7 on behalf of the Home Office and the Department for Communities and Local Government would not have been possible without the help of Building Bridges Burnley, an interfaith group, and the members of the Elm Street Mosque; and I thank them.

I would also like to thank Alison Barr of SPCK for her early encouragement and support. And especial thanks go to my wife Veronica who, as well as debating these issues with me, has patiently endured early mornings of writing for six months – in between moving house, fighting an election and getting married.

Alan Billings
Sheffield

Introduction

If you ask the proverbial man or woman in the street whether religion contributes for good or ill towards the cohesiveness of society, much would depend on what the word 'religion' brought to the forefront of their mind; the evidence is mixed. On the one hand they might acknowledge that religion teaches people to be good neighbours and to care for the sick and the vulnerable. As a result it has inspired many agencies for good – the hospice movement, the Samaritans, soup kitchens for the homeless. On the other hand they might recall that doctors involved in abortions have been killed in the name of religion, and many contemporary conflicts have had a religious dimension if not cause – from Kosovo to the West Bank. If anything, as a result of the attack on the twin towers in New York and the bombs on the London transport system, the balance of public opinion has tilted towards the latter: religion spells trouble. John Gray, for example, has written about the 'atmosphere of moral panic' that currently surrounds religion. Whereas at one time it might have been dismissed as a declining force, now 'it is demonised as the cause of many of the world's worst evils'. As a result, there has been 'a sudden explosion in the literature of proselytizing atheism'.[1]

Until relatively recently government took the view that faith was a private matter and not its concern. As a result, as a previous Home Secretary wrote, 'the record of Government engagement with faith communities has been patchy'.[2] It was assumed that the issues that went to the heart of social and community cohesion were largely to do with tensions and inequalities caused by differences of ethnicity, gender, culture, relative wealth and social class. Although these factors remain significant, there is now a much greater appreciation of the role of faith in framing the identity and influencing the values, attitudes and behaviour not just of individuals but of whole communities. This has prompted questions about how a society remains cohesive if it consists of an increasing number of different faith groups with their various theologies, values and aspirations, as well as a growing constituency that rejects all religion. While this shift of focus on the part of government predated the disturbances in some northern cities (principally Bradford, Burnley and Oldham) in 2001 and the terrorist bombs in London in 2005, those events were seen to have a faith dimension and have proved decisive. As a result, the issue of faith could not be set aside but had to be part of any analysis and solution. There is now a general recognition that we need to be as clear as we can about the extent to which faith contributes, or could contribute, towards underpinning or undermining the cohesiveness of communities in contemporary Britain.

But 'faith' is not an easy matter for government or public bodies to handle. It is made more testing by the fact that modern Britain is as multifaith as any nation on the planet. Public bodies and public servants in the UK are confronted by people from all the major world faiths, with their different beliefs, practices and traditions.[3] London alone has people from over 40 national or ethnic groups, speaking over 300 languages and embracing every variety of religious faith. This requires a degree of knowledge, understanding (religious literacy) and sensitivity on the part of those who have to deal with people from those different faith groups that would be hard to achieve in any circumstances, but more so when tensions are running high or when some of the leading voices in the academic world and the media are hostile towards any religion. In addition, the faiths themselves are not at the same point of maturity or embeddedness in British society. Christianity has been present in Europe for at least fifteen hundred years, influencing every aspect of life and making a major contribution to the emergence of modern Britain. Despite growing secularization, Britain remains a recognizably 'Christian' country in the way that Turkey is recognizably 'Islamic'.[4]

Until relatively recently, it was taken for granted that being British entailed at least nominal adherence to the Christian faith. Few had to think about what it meant to be British and a member of another faith. The exception to that would be the Jewish community. Jews have a long history of working out what it is to be part of a minority faith within a predominantly non-Jewish society and culture.[5] But other faiths are still at the earliest stages of that process.[6] We should not underestimate the distance that British Muslims, for example, have yet to travel. Nor should we underestimate the anxieties within the Christian constituency (that is, from those who declared themselves Christian in the 2001 National Census) as it reluctantly begins to contemplate a future that is characterized by more numerous, more confident and possibly more assertive secular and religious alternatives. This Christian constituency, still numerically large, is beginning to sense a serious weakening of some of its previous power and privilege, and when that happens to groups, they lose confidence and sometimes become less neighbourly.

All of this raises the question of how a society that has such a bewildering array of cultures, ethnicities and religions is able to hold together. How is social and community cohesion to be forged? That is the first question with which I shall be concerned. But running alongside this is the question of religion, and specifically whether religion is a help or hindrance to cohesion.

These issues have interested me during the whole of my life – as a priest in a multifaith parish in inner-city Sheffield in the 1970s; as a city councillor in Leicester and Sheffield over 15 years; as a member of the government's Community Cohesion Panel set up to learn the lessons of the urban riots of 2001; as a researcher into the contribution that interfaith activity was making to community cohesion in North-West towns in 2007.

I have focused on Christianity and Islam, with only passing references to other faiths. The reason for this is in part because the argument I am making can be made without trying to say something about every religion, but also because although all the other faiths are only tiny percentages of the population, Muslims account for more than half of all the non-Christian religions. Even within the Islamic community, I mainly refer to Muslims from a Pakistani background – the community I know best.

I begin by noting that there have been a number of times in recent history when the cohesiveness of British society has been severely tested. Most of these occasions had little to do with religion. But the terrorist outrages of 7 July 2005 were religiously inspired, and this made the government's search for policies that would promote cohesion seem all the more urgent (Chapter 1). This then leads to a consideration of the contribution religion can play in strengthening cohesion (Chapter 2). I then turn to some research I participated in at Lancaster University between 2005 and 2007 that was looking at the consequences for cohesion of the way white (mainly Christian) and Asian (mainly Muslim) groups in some North-West towns lead parallel lives. Does this 'enclavization' set back the cause of cohesion

(Chapter 3)? This is followed by considering whether religion is as beneficial for society as believers claim. A number of recent issues involving religion have led some critics to suggest that far from helping cohesion, religion undermines it (Chapter 4). In a concluding chapter, I seek to draw all of this together by reflecting on the circumstances in which religion could have a helpful role in making communities and the nation more cohesive, and the circumstances in which religion could only be a disintegrating force. Finally, I shall argue that we stand at a tipping point. Religion can be a potent force for bringing communities together. It can equally be a force for setting neighbour against neighbour. My argument is that its future role depends on its willingness to explore what it means to accept that we live now and always in a plural world.

1

Why 'community cohesion'?

---◆◆◆---

The Government's vision for Britain is one of strong, confident communities where local people of all different backgrounds get on well together. That is why building cohesion is a priority for my department.

> *Hazel Blears MP, Secretary of State for Communities*
> *and Local Government*

The issue of religious faith will be of the same significance to the twenty-first century as political ideology was to the twentieth century. In an era of globalization there is nothing more important than getting people of different faiths and therefore cultures to understand each other better and live in peace and mutual respect; and to give faith itself its proper place in the future.

> *Tony Blair, former Prime Minister*

The question, 'What makes communities cohesive?' was not one that occupied the British people in the first few years after the Second World War. It would not have crossed anyone's mind to suppose that either their local community or the nation as a whole was not socially cohesive, even though it was divided by a fairly rigid class system: George Orwell said Britain was 'the most class-ridden country under the sun'.[1] Yet by the beginning of the present century, building 'community cohesion' had become an overriding concern at both national and local level.[2] What has made 'community cohesion' a matter of such importance today?

In this chapter, I will try to set the matter in some historical context by suggesting, first, that there is nothing new about feeling that social and community cohesion is under threat. Over the past 60 years the unity of many communities and the nation as a whole has been challenged many times by social, political and industrial unrest, and perhaps in dynamic economies and vibrant democracies this is to be expected as people struggle with or against or for change. As this

1

period is largely coterminous with my own life, I shall seek to illustrate this in part by reference to events that I lived through and sometimes participated in at first hand. But I shall then suggest that the current concern over cohesiveness is in one significant respect different from what has happened before, in that in addition to some of these familiar themes there is now a religious dimension, and this raises issues of a different kind.

In the period since the Second World War, Britain has become a highly plural society with sizeable communities of ethnic minorities, principally as a result of mass inward migration. Since difference can lead to conflict, the attention of government naturally focused on what at first was the most obvious difference between the host community and the new arrivals – the colour of people's skin. The assumption was that if racial discrimination could be tackled, cohesiveness could be maintained. But more recently, as immigrant communities became settled ethnic minorities, while racial discrimination has by no means been rooted out and can still be a cause of unrest, many in the majority community began to look beyond skin colour and reacted with suspicion and hostility towards what they regarded as the alien religions that immigration had brought. At first, there had been a rather lazy assumption that while newcomers might belong to different religions, faith probably had no greater significance for their lives than it had, seemingly, for the lives of the majority of British people. In any case, a plurality of religious beliefs did not matter to wider society; people could believe anything they liked. What did matter was how they behaved, and here, it was assumed, all religions said something similar; all essentially advocated a version of the golden rule: do to others as you would be done by. After all, this was the message of faith leaders; it was the message of the interfaith movement; it was what was taught in schools; it was the stock-in-trade of speakers on BBC Radio 4's 'Thought for the Day'. (We could say that none of these prepared us for what came next.) Then in July 2005 this dream of different communities living together like the lion and the lamb in some new Eden of communal harmony and tranquillity was swept away when a group of young men took themselves onto the London transport system and detonated bombs, killing both themselves and over 50 of their fellow passengers in the name of religion. As a consequence we were compelled to think more deeply about the place of religion in society. We were forced to recognize that for many people, religion is at the very centre of their understanding of who they are. After family, it was the next most important thing that many among the ethnic minorities said mattered to them – it was far more important than race – and this was especially true of the younger generation, aged 16–24 years.[3] We also came to understand that different religions, and different versions of different religions, give rise to different ways of looking at the world, different values and different ethical norms – and these are not always compatible. This created quite new anxieties: it suggested that even if violent religious extremism could be overcome, a religiously plural society might be difficult to hold together. We had absorbed enough Durkheimian sociology to believe that a society expressed its core values through its religion, but if there were a plurality of religions that might indicate a plurality of fundamental convictions. How long would the cohesion of the nation survive if it could not develop among its citizens a core of shared beliefs and values?

This is one reason for 'community cohesion' becoming such a central issue for government and nation, and why a major component of that is anxiety around religion. The question I address throughout these chapters is, therefore: 'Does religion (and religious pluralism) threaten community cohesion?'

Community cohesion in historical perspective

Let me first outline some of those occasions since the Second World War when social and community cohesion was severely strained. If we return to the immediate post-war period, the reason the nation did not feel any lack of cohesion, despite class differences, was in large measure due to the fact that during the war all social groups had come together to face a common enemy – Nazi Germany – and all had made sacrifices in the interests of the country as a whole. Then, once the conflict was over, there was a universal determination to retain this sense of being one nation by building a fairer and more just society. This is why Atlee's socialists and not Churchill's Conservatives were swept to power in the landslide election of 1945. The egalitarian creed of the Labour Party better encapsulated this general mood, and the Labour Government immediately set about tackling the 'five giants' – want, disease, squalor, ignorance, idleness – that William Beveridge had identified during the war as the principal

3

ills afflicting the country. They legislated first for a major reform of education, and committed the government to provide employment for all; then in 1948 they set up the National Health Service, 'free at the point of need', paid for from the public purse. The benefits of victory and a renewed economic life were to be shared more fairly. My parents' generation, therefore, thought they were building Jerusalem for everyone in the green and pleasant land that was Great Britain.[4]

For the moment, however, most people were only too thankful to live life as they had done before the interruption of the war, and that meant remaining relatively deferential to one's 'betters' and being content in the place you were: your community was your destiny. Lorna Sage captures this well in her memoir of life in rural Hanmer in the 1940s:

> But this was a village where it seemed everybody was their vocation. They didn't just 'know their place', it was as though the place occupied them, so that they knew what they were going to be from the beginning.[5]

We might note that while the sort of community that Lorna Sage describes was certainly cohesive, cohesion was achieved at the expense of any ambition to be different. After the war, the continuing cohesiveness of British society would be guaranteed by a gradual return to full employment and the creation of a welfare state that would care for people 'from the cradle to the grave'. This would more than ameliorate the poverty and deprivation that still persisted, and through national insurance contributions and income tax everyone would contribute to the common good. This was 'loving your neighbour' at a distance – social cohesion based on neighbour-love operating through politics and taxation.[6] Maintaining the welfare state eventually emerged as the political consensus, for while Labour may have brought about the greatest changes in its immediate post-war administrations, the Conservatives did not demolish those achievements when they came to power in 1951 but rather consolidated them. But this post-war settlement sowed seeds of aspiration and ambition as well: social cohesion based on the status quo was about to be undermined.

I was one of the beneficiaries of all this. I was born into a relatively poor working-class family in an East Midlands industrial town during the war, and grew up in the later 1940s and 1950s.[7] My father, who saw active service in North Africa, was not demobilized until 1947, when he resumed work in the final assembly department of the Imperial Typewriter Company. He was an unskilled manual worker who made ends meet by working long hours of overtime. He left for work before I got up in the morning and returned home just before I went to bed at night. My mother also worked full-time; at weekends my father tended his allotment. There was always help at hand for after-school childcare from the family next door or relatives a few streets away. We were part of an extensive network of family and neighbour relationships. Although my father hoped I would follow him into the factory – he even showed me at the age of ten the bench where I would start my working life – my mother was inspired by the post-war changes to be more aspirational – not for herself (she had left school at 14), but for her children. She was determined that I should be able to take advantage of the post-war educational settlement. This was why she worked. I passed the 'eleven-plus' and went to the grammar school and then university on a state scholarship.[8] This more than covered my living expenses and, unlike the graduates of today, I left Cambridge with a small surplus that enabled me to get married! More to the point, I did not doubt that if anyone wanted to move up the social ladder, had the ability and set their mind to it, they could do so.[9] For post-war Britain was meritocratic Britain. I left university a convinced meritocratic socialist and joined the Labour Party. This was where I placed the emphasis in Clause Four of the Labour Party's constitution. The key for me was not common ownership but securing 'for the workers by hand or by brain the full fruits of their industry'.[10]

When people speak nostalgically about the demise of community and politicians, and clergy laud the virtues of community, I often think back to my working-class origins. The community was very supportive – when people fell ill or on hard times, or loved ones died, for example. But it could also be very cruel. 'Rough children', gay men, unmarried mothers, unmarried couples – divorce was expensive and difficult to obtain – were ruthlessly shunned, as was anyone who strayed from the accepted norms of custom and conduct in countless other respects.[11] When a family of gypsies moved into the street they were not visited or encouraged to join local clubs, and we children were warned not to play with them. My mother, who in all other respects was the most hospitable and charitable of people, said gypsies could not be trusted not to steal children. We learnt the skipping verse:

> My mother said that I never should
> Play with gypsies in the wood,
> The wood was dark; the grass was green;
> In came Sally with a tambourine,
> I went to the sea – no ship to get across,
> I paid ten shillings for a blind white horse;
> I up on his back and was off in a crack,
> Sally, tell my mother I shall never come back.

Richard Layard has written about the correlation between enjoying frequent interaction through close community life and individual happiness, which I am sure is true.[12] But I found this working-class community stifling and oppressive. It was something to get away from, and the meritocratic educational system was my escape. Among the undoubted effects of the greater affluence and social mobility of these years were the loosening of community ties and an increased individualism.

But meritocracy and equality of opportunity are not the same as equality, and many on the political left thought they were incompatible. A meritocratic society seems inimical to egalitarianism since it works by enabling those who have abilities to develop them and rewarding them for their achievements. The grammar-school system, whatever its flaws, was the educational route whereby that merit was discovered and nurtured, enabling young people from poor homes and less privileged backgrounds to flourish. It is arguable that the goal of equality has to be pursued not directly but indirectly, and that the period of British history that was most meritocratic was also the most egalitarian in terms of the distribution of income and wealth. This is probably because as well as being meritocratic there was also a strong emphasis on looking after those who fell by the way – the elderly, the sick, the unemployed. This was the contribution that socialism (informed by the nonconformist conscience) made to meritocracy. But those who saw meritocracy as 'unsocialist' in itself believed that it simply created new inequalities based on ability rather than inherited privilege, and spent much of the 1970s and 1980s unnecessarily unpicking the post-war educational settlement: the big comprehensive school was the result. The paradox was that the country became more, not less, economically and socially divided. The divide between meritocratic and egalitarian socialists remained unresolved in the Labour Party and smouldered away until Tony Blair forced the issue in 1995, when Clause Four was effectively abandoned and New Labour – which promised equality of opportunity rather than egalitarianism – was born.[13] What New Labour essentially wanted was an enabling state – the phrase was Neil Kinnock's – rather than a paternalistic state that did everything for you or a laissez-faire state that simply left people to their individual choices and fate. In fact the older class system proved stubbornly enduring alongside new hierarchies based on merit. But as long as the routes out of poverty were expanding (through hard work or education), Britain's class system, old and new, did not cause undue resentment or social instability.

Britain remained a cohesive society in the immediate post-war years because there was a general acceptance that the values that essentially united the nation were Christian. This is what the war had been about. As Churchill said in 1940, when it seemed as though Hitler was poised to invade: 'The Battle of Britain is about to begin. Upon this battle depends the survival of Christian civilization.' Churchill was not particularly religious, but like many members of the establishment at that time he deemed it prudent not to say so; he said he was a flying buttress to the national Church, supporting it from the outside.[14] After the war, a new enemy soon appeared that gave a continuing reason to defend Christianity – the atheist Soviet Union. One consequence of the collapse of communism in the 1980s was that it made it easier for people to attack religion in the West.

We were also becoming better off, and communities that feel economically confident are likely to be more cohesive. The first television appeared in our street in 1953. Mr and Mrs Woodward, who sold and repaired bicycles, bought a small set with a nine-inch screen, and invited neighbours to watch the coronation of the young Queen Elizabeth. We sat round peering at grainy images through a large lens positioned in front of the set to magnify (and distort!) the picture. In 1955 over one-third of the population had televisions, but by 1975 this had risen to 96 per cent.[15]

This picture of neighbours gathered around a television to mark the coronation is a reminder that Britain also had a powerful focus of unity in the monarchy and those commemorations at which the monarch presided – such as the annual Act of Remembrance each November at the Cenotaph. (These are the nearest we get to such national celebrations as Independence and Thanksgiving in the USA or Bastille Day in France.) The Royal Family was popular at the end of the war as a result of the decision of the King and Queen to stay in London throughout hostilities and not retreat to the safety of Canada. This, and their frequent visits to munitions factories and bomb sites, meant that they were held in great affection. I have an early childhood memory of the head teacher of my primary school coming into an assembly in 1952 to announce that the King (George VI) had died. We all burst into tears.

When Gordon Brown became Prime Minister in 2007, he was much exercised with the question of creating a sense of national – British – identity, and Lord Goldsmith was asked to find ways of doing this. Eyes were cast in the direction of the USA, where young people pledge allegiance to the national flag each morning. But this was widely derided as something the British do not do. In the light of this, the existence of the monarchy as a focus of national unity should not be underestimated. Because it already exists, it does not have to be argued for – though it can be argued against and lost.

Threats to cohesion

But from the 1960s onwards, social tensions began to arise between different ethnic groups as traditional white, working-class towns and cities began to absorb successive waves of largely non-white Commonwealth immigrants whose labour Britain needed in factories, the transport system and the National Health Service. The government sought to combat racism with legislation making racial discrimination an offence. But one Conservative shadow minister, Enoch Powell, warned in a highly emotive speech to the West Midlands Conservative Political Centre in 1968 that unless immigration were not just stopped but actually reversed, the social cohesiveness of local communities and the nation as a whole would be irreparably damaged. The crux of the argument seemed to be that the concentration of large numbers of immigrants in certain areas of urban Britain made successful integration into British society impossible. Some, he believed, did not want to integrate. The example he gave was of increasing demands by some ethnic minority groups – he mentioned Sikhs – for some of their alien customs and traditions to be accommodated to British practices or allowed special exemptions in British law. (He was probably referring to requests from Sikh bus conductors in Wolverhampton to be allowed to wear their turbans and not the regulation peaked cap. This seems relatively trivial now, but then it was an issue that generated a great deal of heat. It was felt that the issue of turbans was just the thin end of a potentially very big wedge.) One of Powell's biographers, Robert Shepherd, has suggested that what Powell feared was the 'communalism' he had encountered while on active service in India during the war. There each political party was dominated by one or other communal group – Hindu, Muslim, Sikh, Dalit – and seemed unable to rise above sectional interest.[16] Powell feared for the homogeneity of the British electorate. It stirred uncomfortable memories of the serious race riots that had erupted in the USA just a few years before and that we had all witnessed on television.[17] A former professor of Greek, he ended his speech by warning of trouble ahead with a highly charged classical reference. He said that 'Like the Roman,' he seemed to see 'the River Tiber foaming with much blood' – it became known as the 'Rivers of blood' speech.

Powell divided the nation. The wife of one of his closest friends, who was also the editor of his local paper, disowned him.[18] The political classes were unanimous in their condemnation: they thought it was simply racist or gave succour to racists. Edward Heath, the Conservative leader, removed Powell from his shadow cabinet. But many white working-class people felt that he was articulating some of their own fears. Dock workers in London even stopped work for a day and marched to Parliament in support of him. Some carried posters that read, 'Back Britain not Black Britain'. The Labour MP for Poplar, Ian Mikardo, who argued with the dockers, was kicked. A Gallup Poll revealed that 74 per cent of people agreed with Powell and 83 per cent felt that immigration should be restricted.[19] *Plus ça change.*

The tragedy of Enoch Powell's speech was that by using inflammatory language he made it impossible for anyone else to speak publicly about the important issues of immigration and integration without appearing to support racists. In turn, this also paralysed public consideration of the wider question about how any society in the modern world can be both plural and cohesive. Debate was closed down for almost 40 years. This was potentially even more damaging for race relations and the longer-term issue of how mass immigration was to be handled in ways that safeguarded social and community cohesion.[20]

I was a curate in Leicester at this time, and between 1970 and 1973 a Labour member of the city council. They were years marked by considerable racial tension, coming to a head in 1972, when General Idi Amin, the President of Uganda, gave the Asian population 90 days to leave the country. Thousands fled, many to Britain, and particularly to Leicester. But the city council, Labour and Conservative alike, sought to have the refugees turned back, and those of us who spoke out against this bi-partisan policy, appealing to fellow councillors to prepare for their coming, found ourselves the object of hate mail and unpleasant telephone calls. After one highly charged debate, as I left the Town Hall, which had been picketed by extreme right-wing groups, I was physically attacked by members of the National Front. The police inspector to whom I appealed for help said, 'What do you expect with views like yours?' Looking back 30 years later it is hard to recapture how tense the city was at that time. The irony was that of all the Asian groups that have migrated to the UK, the twice-displaced Ugandan Asians are among the more economically successful. They were businessmen, small shopkeepers and professionals, full of entrepreneurial spirit, who went on to make substantial contributions to the economic and cultural life of the city and the nation.

For many years, racial issues and the question of immigration dominated local and national politics, and from time to time seriously threatened community cohesion in cities like Leicester. When race riots erupted in Brixton and other inner-city areas in 1980 and 1981, it seemed like a vindication of Powell's prophetic warning. Those disturbances had their immediate origins in poor relationships between the police and largely Afro-Caribbean young people in deprived areas, especially with regard to police powers of stop-and-search, which the black community felt was disproportionately directed against them. The subsequent Scarman report, although about Brixton, raised issues common to all the places of disturbance.[21] It spoke of serious racial disadvantage, especially in housing and employment. At the time of these riots, and against a background of national recession, unemployment in Brixton stood at 13 per cent, but among black young people it was estimated to be as high as 55 per cent.

But in the event, the principal anxiety of the period – which also contributed to racial tensions – was the return of high levels of unemployment. An international oil crisis began in 1973, precipitating inflation and recession across Europe. Hostility to foreign workers increased and in many countries there were attempts to limit immigration altogether.[22] Both West Germany and France banned workers from outside the European Economic Community, and France and Switzerland attempted to stop dependents as well – Switzerland with some success. But immigrant labour continued to be needed for those jobs that white British workers were not prepared to undertake.

Industrial life in Britain during the 1970s was punctuated by a series of damaging strikes and the actions of one particular trade union spokesman, Derek Robinson – dubbed 'red Robbo' by the popular press – seemed to sum it all up. As the union convenor for British Leyland at the Longbridge works in Birmingham, he is credited with causing 523 strikes and walkouts in just over one year. By the early 1980s almost four million people were unemployed, and the country seemed to divide ever more sharply between those with a job and those without. Many of those who were laid off in the traditional 'smoke-stack' industries of the Midlands and the North were precisely the Afro-Caribbean and Asian workers who had been taken on to meet labour shortages after the war. The Prime Minister of the day, Margaret Thatcher, said that unemployment was the price that had to be paid if the British economy were to be restructured. This was in some contrast to all her predecessors, Conservative as well as Labour, who had lived through the unemployment of the 1920s and 1930s and saw it as the greatest of scourges.[23] Industrial strife became increasingly frequent and social cohesion at times looked quite precarious. It did not help that some of the political rhetoric of the time seemed harsh and unfeeling – such as Norman Tebbit's advice to the unemployed following the urban riots of 1981: 'I grew up in the '30s with an unemployed father. He didn't riot. He got on his bike and looked for work, and he kept looking 'til he found it.'[24]

The language of class warfare was heard again, not least during disputes with the miners in 1973–4 and more particularly in the year-long miners' strike, 1984–5. The Prime Minister in 1973–4 was Edward Heath, who went to the country for a mandate to settle the issue of 'Who governs Britain?' – the government or the trade unions. He lost the election and the question was left hanging in the air. But when Margaret Thatcher replaced Heath as Conservative leader, she knew that the restructuring of the economy was going to lead to further confrontations, and this time there had to be pre-planning to ensure the government was not successfully challenged. The 1984–5 miners' strike was called to try to resist pit closures as the country moved away from using coal to meet its energy needs – or bought cheap coal from abroad. The rhetoric of the mineworkers' leader, Arthur Scargill, frequently expanded the significance of the struggle to one of the whole of the working class against those who controlled capital. The miners were to be the advance guard of the socialist revolution – rather as the Bolsheviks had been in the Russian revolution of 1917.

By this time I was a parish priest in Sheffield and deputy leader of the city council. Arthur Scargill and Mick McGahey, the Scottish mineworkers' leader, came to meetings in Sheffield Town Hall from time to time as we sought ways for the city council to assist South Yorkshire miners and their families, who faced growing hardship as the strike dragged on. I witnessed at first hand quite extraordinary scenes as miners and police engaged in daily battles across the Yorkshire coalfields. Each morning, police vans full of officers from all over the country gathered in the streets behind my vicarage before setting off for that day's confrontation with strikers. It was a time of very great tension. The country polarized, for or against the striking miners. This often made the pastoral task of the clergy difficult in mining areas. One of my colleagues, a priest with two pits in the parish, had in his congregation a police sergeant, a mine deputy (part of the management), striking miners and non-striking miners – and their families. These divisions were replicated in churches and clubs across the coalfields, creating bitter disputes between and sometimes within families. Some of those quarrels are remembered to this day. The churches tended to sympathize with the strikers, especially as the days lengthened and striking miners and their families began to struggle financially. But Mrs Thatcher called the National Union of Mineworkers 'the enemy within'.[25] If ever there was a time in post-war Britain when social cohesion seemed to be seriously threatened, it must have been during the period of the strike.

It was against this background of heightened tensions and industrial decay that I helped to produce in 1985 a Church of England report, *Faith in the City*, that pointed to the way we were creating ghettos of deprivation – we called them 'urban priority areas' – not just in mining areas but wherever manufacturing industry was in decline or collapse.[26] This was hardly the Jerusalem to which my parents had looked forward 40 years before.

One of the reasons the National Union of Mineworkers gave for opposing mine closures was the effect it would have on community cohesion – though the term was not then used. The whole life of the coalfield communities revolved around the pits and the social clubs associated with them. They provided employment and recreation and sustained local economies. When a pit closed, the effect on the community was dramatic: pubs and clubs, shops and post offices closed; even the colliery band was affected. One of the arguments of the trade unions was that economic and industrial policy had to serve the ends of community – something no government could ever accept, unless it wanted to destroy the national economy. Nevertheless, the consequences for communities of the collapse of a major industry was an important issue, and not one whose implications the government had completely understood. There were few policies to meet the developing situation of community disintegration in the older industrial areas.

For a brief period during this industrial turmoil, people wondered whether Britain had become 'ungovernable'. But it was only for a time. Once Mrs Thatcher had faced down the trade unions there was never any really serious questioning of the cohesiveness of British society, even though the Prime Minister was forced to acknowledge the need to 'do something about the inner cities' after the 1981 racially motivated disturbances. In other words, even she recognized that cohesion had been shaken as a result of social disadvantage, economic restructuring and racial discrimination. But the sense of ungovernability did briefly return in 1990 when Mrs Thatcher's government introduced a new and very unpopular tax – the Community Charge, or poll tax. This led to acts of civil disobedience in several towns, though especially in the capital, when some 200,000 people sought to converge on Trafalgar Square. The protest was unwieldy and violent. The Prime Minister's authority and judgement were called in question, and by the end of the year she had resigned.

To many people the Thatcher years did seem very turbulent. But by 1997, when Tony Blair's New Labour Party swept to power, there was an optimism about the future of the country that was not unlike that enjoyed by the incoming Labour Government of Clement Attlee in 1945. Social cohesion did not seem to be in doubt: building Jerusalem was back on the political agenda.

Northern Ireland

However, there was one part of the UK where from the 1960s onwards social and community cohesion was continuously threatened – Northern Ireland. Although 'the troubles' were frequently referred to as a dispute between 'Protestants' and 'Catholics', the underlying issues in the Province were essentially about a political disagreement between nationalists and loyalists and the social and economic injustice meted out to the former by the latter. The conflict – *pace* Ian Paisley – was never really *about* religion, though religion was used as a marker of difference by the two communities – something I will come back to in a later chapter. But the solution was decidedly political. However, for 30 years, Northern Ireland was a divided community and from time to time the conflict there spilled across to the mainland and caused tensions here between Irish people and their neighbours.

The urban riots of 2001

Yet a few years into the new century, with the Irish question being resolved and despite a thriving economy and unprecedented prosperity, the matter of community cohesion was widely seen as one of the most urgent social issues facing the government and the nation as a whole. What had happened? Why was the social cohesion of the country thought to be so threatened when more people were in work, more people owned their own homes, more young people were going to university than ever before and when so much had been done to overcome racism and other forms of discrimination in every area of life?

The short answer is that there was a growing perception – though it was not often or easily articulated – that in some parts of the country communities of mainly Muslim Asians had grown up that were not integrating in the way (it was thought) other ethnic and religious groups had done in the past. Unlike the Afro-Caribbean communities, the Asian communities from the subcontinent often spoke another language, dressed differently and practised a religion about which most Britons were profoundly ignorant. Ignorance produces fear.

Anxieties had first surfaced in 1988, when Salman Rushdie's novel, *The Satanic Verses*, was published. The title is a reference to a contentious text in the Qur'an that Rushdie interpreted to mean that the Prophet Muhammad, in an attempt to win over the people of Mecca, had once been tempted by the devil into speaking favourably about three of their local female deities.[27] Since Islam considers idolatry the greatest sin, this was tantamount to saying that, for whatever reason, Muhammad was once tempted towards idolatry.[28] The book caused outrage among Muslim communities not only in the UK but across the Islamic world. Ayatollah Ruhollah Khomenei, the supreme Leader of Iran, issued a condemnatory *fatwa* that made the killing of Rushdie a religious duty. The book was burnt in the street by Sunni Muslims in Bradford. Statements were made by those opposed to Rushdie – whose family were Shia Muslims – denouncing the idea of freedom of speech. This, the terms of the *fatwa* and the subsequent treatment of Rushdie were regarded by most people as abhorrent. In 1989, Mustafa Mahmoud Mazeh tried to kill Rushdie with a bomb in London, but the device went off prematurely, killing Mazeh and destroying two floors of a hotel in Paddington. Serious worries about Islam were beginning to form. Then in 2001 two unrelated events took place in the UK and in the USA that together gave added momentum to these fears – the summer disturbances in Bradford, Oldham and Burnley by Asian youths and the terrorist attacks on New York and Washington by a group of Muslim men.

Throughout May, June and July 2001 there were riots in a number of northern English towns. For several nights, gangs of mainly Pakistani young men set cars and buildings on fire and attacked the police. In this respect they were not unlike the riots of the mainly black young people in Bristol, London, Birmingham, Manchester and

Liverpool in 1980 and 1981. Even so, despite the similarities, the disturbances in Yorkshire and the North West in 2001 seemed to point to something more fundamentally troubling. Among other things, some of those convicted and imprisoned were in employment (though by no means all), were married and had supportive families. Explaining the riots in terms of deprivation alone did not seem to capture everything. Unspoken questions began to form: was there something about the religion and culture of the Muslim Asian communities that made integration not just difficult but impossible? Perhaps they did not want to integrate. A general mood of anxiety and unease was created.

In a report for the government on all the 2001 disturbances, Ted Cantle spoke of deprived and impoverished communities but also of deeply fractured communities – whites and Asians, living side by side yet in complete ignorance of one another.[29] He said they lived 'parallel lives', as a result of which communities were in danger of losing 'cohesion'. The Cantle report introduced the idea of 'community cohesion' to the UK, adapting the Canadian idea of 'social cohesion', and Ted Cantle was appointed to chair a Community Cohesion Panel that sought to distil key messages from people's experience of multicultural Britain and to make recommendations to government.[30] I was a member, and became joint chair of the Faith Practitioners group. Unlike social cohesion (though the terms are now often used interchangeably), community cohesion had a more localized focus. It suggested that if people of different ethnicities, cultures and faiths were to live together in towns and cities with any sense of mutuality, they had to get to know more about each other and share some common attitudes. Without some core of shared values and some interaction, people might live in the same town but that town would not be a cohesive community. The disturbances of 2001 were to be regarded as a wake-up call to the nation. They suggested that communities were developing in urban centres across the country in ways that were increasingly less cohesive. Cantle, therefore, made one of his principal recommendations the adoption by government of the idea of community cohesion as a central objective of public policy. The government accepted the Cantle report. It believed that community cohesion was at serious risk, and government policies had to address that as a matter of urgency. Since that time, every government department, every local authority, every state school, every primary care trust and every housing association, and many other public bodies or publicly funded bodies, have pursued a 'community cohesion agenda'. But what the various reports and responses were more cautious and muted about was the role of religion in all of this, though the perpetrators of the summer riots had been identified as 'Muslims' – which was also the religion of those who flew the planes into the twin towers and the Pentagon in America on September 11, 2001, killing 3,000 people. But before turning to the question of religion, a word needs to be said about the idea of community cohesion.

The erosion of cohesion

The issue of community cohesion is not just about different ethnic and religious groups living parallel lives. Trends in modern societies were already contributing towards lack of cohesion, as Ferdinand Tönnies pointed out in his classic comparison of communities before and after the industrial revolution. Tönnies distinguished two types of community, which he called *Gemeinschaft* and *Gesellschaft*.[31] Before the industrial revolution, individuals were bound together by kinship, by working together and by sharing a common faith, common values and common traditions and customs. There was also frequent interaction – *Gemeinschaft*. People did not have to think about making their community cohesive – it just was. A shared understanding – what Goran Rosenberg called the 'warm circle'[32] – was simply taken for granted. The circle was 'warm' precisely because it was taken for granted. Belonging was not something that had to be worked at or thought about: you simply 'belonged'. All that that did for shared understanding passes unnoticed. Communities of this sort began to disappear with the coming of factories and the growth of towns.

In modern, urban and industrial society, what bound people together were the networks of friendships that came about through work and found expression in organizations such as trade unions, political parties, the Co-operative Guild, working men's clubs, the Buffaloes, churches and other voluntary societies – *Gesellschaft*. These organizations served to mediate the relationship of the individual to the state, local and national, and promoted moral frameworks within which communities made sense of the world and ordered their collective lives. The point that Tönnies makes was also made in the nineteenth century by the French social commentator Alexis de Tocqueville. Reflecting on a visit to the USA, and being impressed by its vibrancy, he wondered what a society needed for its social health. He concluded that it depended on there being a critical mass of citizens involved in voluntary associations – what he called 'the little platoons'.[33] Americans, he found, belonged to 'a thousand different types' of associations '... religious, moral, serious, futile, very general and very limited, immensely large and very minute'.[34]

Since the late 1950s, voluntary bodies of all kinds have been in decline, and so communities of this sort have been disappearing too.[35] In other words, community cohesion is under threat from a number of different directions. It is not just about trying to integrate different ethnic and cultural groups that at the moment are living side by side with little contact between them. Even without that, modern society does not generate the clubs, societies and informal networks that lead to social interaction. The more prosperous we are, the more we seek individual rather than communitarian satisfactions. Community seems to be in part a function of poverty. What Ted Cantle and others found in northern towns with their ethnic divisions, the result of immigration, is but a further factor in communities losing something of their past cohesiveness.

For all these reasons, community cohesion became a central concern of government at the beginning of the new century. But what exactly is a 'cohesive community' in multiracial, multiethnic and multifaith Britain?

Defining community cohesion

There have been various attempts to say what a cohesive community is and to define 'community cohesion' (I will return to this in the final chapter). The Local Government Association (LGA), for example, summarized it for its members (local authorities) in 2002 with a four-point test. A cohesive community is one where:

- there is a common vision and a sense of belonging for all communities;
- the diversity of people's different backgrounds and circumstances is appreciated and positively valued;

- those from different backgrounds have similar life opportunities;
- strong and positive relationships are being developed between people from different backgrounds in the workplace, in schools and within neighbourhoods.[36]

When the Commission on Integration and Cohesion – set up in 2007 to report on what was needed to ensure cohesive communities – issued its report, it urged the government to clarify the concept of community cohesion.[37] The government responded with 'a new definition of Community Cohesion' – by this time the term had capital letters – though whether it added clarity is another matter.

> Community Cohesion is what must happen in all communities to enable different groups of people to get on well together. A key contributor to community cohesion is integration, which is what must happen to enable new residents and existing residents to adjust to one another.
>
> Our vision of an integrated and cohesive community is based on three foundations:
>
> - people from different backgrounds having similar life opportunities;
> - people knowing their rights and responsibilities;
> - people trusting one another and trusting local institutions to act fairly.
>
> And three key ways of living together:
>
> - a shared future vision and sense of belonging;
> - a focus on what new and existing communities have in common, alongside a recognition of the value of diversity;
> - strong and positive relationships between people from different backgrounds.[38]

There is something rather odd about this definition as distinct from that of the LGA. The LGA sees community cohesion as an *outcome* of policies and programmes; the government tends to blur this distinction, and it is not always clear whether by community cohesion they are referring to the outcome of policies or the policies themselves. Both definitions stress the need for a 'common' or 'shared future' vision, which is something I shall query in the final chapter. For the moment I will simply say that if this shared vision refers to beliefs and values, then it is a forlorn hope, though in so far as government sets store by it, the existence of religious pluralism would create a major and insuperable problem. Community cohesion cannot be made to depend on people having beliefs and values in common since modern societies are inescapably plural. In the past, states sought cohesion by enforcing common beliefs and values on their populations, but that is not an option for a modern democracy. The issue for us is how (or whether) we can bring social and community cohesion out of pluralism.

The government definition does differ in one significant respect from that of the LGA – the addition of the word 'integration' (the Commission had been charged to look into integration and cohesion). This presumably adds something to 'cohesion' or makes clearer what cohesion means. The government looks for an integrated and not just a cohesive society, or sees increasing integration as the key to social cohesion.

But an integrated society is not the only way in which social cohesion could be achieved. Two other models are possible and have guided social policy in other parts of the world. It is at least arguable that it would be possible to have a cohesive society in which different ethnic, cultural or religious groups were not integrated – a society, for instance, where different groups lived harmonious, equally valued, yet parallel lives. This is one definition of multiculturalism. Canada is an example of a country that has embraced multiculturalism as an official policy – each culture and subculture is affirmed and thought to contribute positively to the life of the whole nation. So, for example, the people of Quebec are able to speak French and live with a degree of autonomy from English-speaking Canada.

It would also be possible for a society to simply 'assimilate' new groups so that newcomers were not encouraged to maintain their own traditions and customs, their culture, but over time merged with the dominant culture, principally through having to speak the language of the host community and through intermarriage. Britain has clearly assimilated many groups of people in this way in the past. The French Protestant Huguenots, who fled ferocious Roman Catholic persecution in the seventeenth century, have long since been assimilated, with only a few Huguenot surnames remaining to remind us of that history. But assimilation through marriage has its consequences, especially for religion: parents have to make a decision about the religious tradition in which they nurture their children, and sometimes that may be resolved by raising them in neither faith, thus contributing towards greater secularization. This is why the Roman Catholic Church has in the past insisted that the children of a mixed marriage should be brought up as Catholics, and why the Chief Rabbi is anxious altogether about Jews 'marrying out'.

But the government has set its face against both parallel lives and assimilation and argues that this understanding of community cohesion as 'integrated' is what 'must happen' because it wants groups of people not just to live amicably side by side but to 'get on well together' and to 'build better relationships' – to be integrated. The shared vision, therefore, must be the vision of an integrated and cohesive society, and the common values must include all that makes for integration. We could see the options for Britain as a continuum running from 'parallel lives' to 'assimilation', with 'integration' somewhere between, though given the anxieties about parallel lives, integration lies nearer to assimilation:

Models of social organization:
Parallel lives—Integration—Assimilation

But what does this mean in practice? Those who, following the riots, produced the reports that recommended community cohesion policies began by pointing to what they saw as the danger: towns where different ethnic, religious and cultural groups were living parallel lives because they lived in separate parts of the town and did not often or easily mix with one another. This is what community cohesion – understood as a set of policies – is intended to break down. At the very least, therefore, as well as continuing with existing policies designed to reduce discrimination, it would include longer-term action designed to achieve more difficult goals such as:

- preventing the development of separate enclaves of people of different ethnicities, religions and cultures;
- encouraging more mixed residential areas;
- supporting regular intercommunity involvement, dialogue and activity;
- preventing the development of separate schools for children of different ethnic, cultural and religious backgrounds (exclusive faith schools would need to be discouraged);

- promoting civic occasions, celebrations and commemorations that bring different groups together;
- discouraging any activities that tend to separate one group from another;
- refusing to support activities that are not open to people of all ethnicities, cultures and religions.

But as soon as we start to lay out what community cohesion might involve in practice we encounter problems; for how would such integrative strategies be consistent with other government objectives? How does the commitment to recognizing and valuing cultural diversity fit with the idea of integration? How can faith schools be discouraged while supporting parental choice? There are at least questions here.

The stakes in all this are very high. What began to push the government in the direction of community cohesion conceived as integration were the summer disturbances. They had caused more anguish than the earlier urban racial riots of 1980 and 1981 (mainly Afro-Caribbean youth) because of the perception that this was not so much a riot about deprivation, lack of opportunity and discriminatory policing as about acceptance and belonging. Or rather it was thought that deprivation, lack of opportunity and discriminatory policing were interpreted by the younger Asian community as a sign of not being accepted. But it was more than this. There was also a fear – though this was spoken *sotto voce* – that the Muslim Asian groups that made up the northern towns might not share the fundamental values of the rest of British society. Some in the white majority felt that the Asian minority were introducing into the country an alien subculture and religion – Islam – that had little or nothing of value to contribute and might even be corrosive of traditional British values; while many in the Asian community felt their religion and culture were not understood, valued or accepted by the white community, some concluding that they could never be accepted. This, it was feared, might be at the root of the disturbances. Better housing, better schools and more jobs might ameliorate this situation, but they would not overcome the perceptions of some among the white majority and the Asian minority that their respective cultures and religions were somehow inimical.

The religious dimension

Then, on 7 July 2005, the fourth anniversary of the Bradford riots, a series of co-ordinated terrorist outrages occurred on the London transport system.[39] Just before nine o'clock in the morning, three bombs were exploded by suicide bombers within a few seconds of one another on three underground trains. A fourth bomb was detonated on a London bus in Tavistock Square about an hour afterwards. The population noted that the bombers gave religious reasons for what they did. One of them, Mohammad Sidique Khan, for example, said in a videotaped message broadcast by al-Jazeera a few weeks later:

> I and thousands like me are forsaking everything for what we believe. Our drive and motivation doesn't come from tangible commodities that this world has to offer. Our religion is Islam, obedience to the one true God and following the footsteps of the final prophet messenger. Your democratically elected governments continuously perpetuate atrocities against my people all over the world. And your support of them makes you directly responsible, just as I am directly responsible for protecting and avenging my Muslim brothers and sisters. Until we feel security you will be our targets and until you stop the bombing, gassing, imprisonment and torture of my people we will not stop this fight. We are at war and I am a soldier. Now you too will taste the reality of this situation.[40]

It was also noted that the British bombers were not people from another country but 'home-grown' terrorists. The bomb factory was quite quickly traced to Leeds. What caused alarm was the way the suicide bombers defined themselves by their religion and seemed to have no particular love for or loyalty to their country.

Other attacks followed in London later in July 2005 – when the bombs failed to explode[41] – and then London and Glasgow in 2007.[42] Some terrorists were apprehended and tried. In the publicity surrounding these failed or foiled plots the British public became increasingly aware of the nature of the extreme politico-theological ideas that motivated the terrorists. They were not just reacting to aspects of British foreign policy. It was also clear that their agendas were more far-reaching than that: the restoration of an Islamic caliphate; the eventual submission of the West to Islam;

and so on. The police and security services indicated that there might be as many as 2,000 people who were giving them cause for alarm. Despite every effort by most Muslims in the country to distance themselves from the bombers and their ideology, anxieties about Islam multiplied. Few believed that the Qur'an instructed Muslims to wage war on unbelievers, but increasing numbers began to wonder whether there was something about the Islamic religion that enabled terrorists to find religious justification a little too easily. Since Islam is not hierarchically organized it was difficult for the Muslim community to produce a spokesman – the equivalent of the Archbishop of Canterbury or Chief Rabbi – who could authoritatively rebut charges or present an authoritative, alternative theological statement – though any number of Muslim clerics made inflammatory pronouncements elsewhere in the world. What seemed to be lacking was any clear theological guidance about how one could be Muslim and British. No one recognized just how deep the anxieties about Islam were becoming in the rest of the population until early in 2008, and even then in the most unexpected way.

In February of that year the Archbishop of Canterbury gave a lecture in which he appeared to argue for Sharia law and Sharia courts to be incorporated into or accommodated to English law.[43] I shall return to this in a later chapter, but for the moment we can note that in the furore that followed the lecture and a radio interview the Archbishop gave beforehand, it became clear that many people believed that some mosques were already attempting to regulate the lives of Muslims according to Sharia. What had been an attempt to make Muslims feel more accepted in British society unleashed a wave of anger that indicated a considerable degree of anxiety and perhaps Islamophobia. Suddenly the ghost of Enoch Powell came into view.

The row exposed a deep contradiction at the heart of government policy. How was it possible on the one hand to encourage diversity – celebrating and supporting different religions and cultures – and on the other to promote community cohesion, understood as integration, when some religions or some versions of some religions did not believe in celebrating or even tolerating diversity and had views and practices of which no British government could conceivably approve? Enabling Sharia to operate in some areas and for some people would be entrenching separate ethnic and religious communities and not integrating them. It undermined community cohesion. I have no doubt that one by-product of all this has been a more general calling into question of the role of religion in public life.

Summary and conclusion

From time to time during my life, community cohesion has been shaken as a result of crises caused, among other things, by industrial unrest, immigration and political terrorism. It has also been threatened by the breakdown of community itself due to the reluctance of increasing numbers of people to play much of a part in civil society. But what has focused attention on the question of how we are to live together in modern Britain has been the gradual recognition of the role that religion plays in the life of at least one substantial minority community. This has forced us to think more urgently about what unites us and the seemingly ambiguous place of religion. Does community cohesion require a bedrock of shared beliefs and values? Does religion and a plurality of religions work for or against cohesion? To these questions we turn in subsequent chapters, beginning with a consideration of the positive contribution that religion makes to community life.

2

The contribution of faith to community cohesion

Whether we believe in God or not, I think most of us have a sense of
the spiritual, that recognition of a deeper meaning and purpose in our
lives, and I believe that this sense flourishes despite the pressures of
our world.   *Queen Elizabeth II*

We commit ourselves,
in a spirit of friendship and co-operation,
to work together
alongside all who share our values and ideals,
to help bring about a better world
now and for generations to come.
                    From A Shared Act of Commitment and Reflection
                                                    (see Appendix 1)

In this chapter I want to ask whether faith communities continue to
make a contribution towards community cohesion and, if they do,
what it is and whether they will be able to continue making it given
the likely future of organized religion. I will do this by first recalling
a world that has all but disappeared in the UK – the close-knit
working-class community – in order to understand better what we
mean by 'community' and 'community cohesion' and the role that
faith groups have played historically.

I was born and brought up just after the Second World War in
a working-class district of Leicester, an East-Midlands industrial
town. Life for my family revolved around four local institutions: the
corner shop (selling groceries and general household goods); some
local factories (principally the Imperial Typewriter Company and
some small boot and shoe works); the local parish church (St
Stephen, East Park Road); and the Dorothy Road Fellowship. The
lives of all our neighbours were similarly focused, though for some

the local public house was also important. The Fellowship was a self-help group founded shortly after the war, with a membership of street residents. It had an annual levy, out of which it organized social activities and did charitable deeds. Almost every household in the street was a member. Each year, for example, the Fellowship arranged a sports day in a local park for parents and children, a winter season of Saturday-night film shows for families and, set in a works canteen, a fancy-dress Christmas party. These were the days before televisions or computers. Each summer there were outings to the Billing Aquadrome and Bradgate Park. One of the biggest single events was the street party to mark the coronation of Queen Elizabeth II. But it was not entirely about enjoyment. When an older person became ill, the members of the Fellowship would take it in turns to do simple nursing, to shop, cook and clean for them. When they were terminally ill members organized a rota to sit with them or their spouse until they died. When that happened, my mother would go and lay out the body – washing and dressing it prior to its removal by the undertaker.[1] A collection would be taken for a wreath and for the widow or widower. The whole street would know when someone died, and as a mark of respect all the curtains facing the pavement would be closed until after the funeral. The Dorothy Road Fellowship was a mini welfare state – 'care in the community' – and so destined to decline as publicly funded welfare provision expanded. Replicated in many other streets across the city, it was not unique. What was so important about all of them was that everything was planned and delivered by the local residents themselves. In this way these working-class neighbourhoods built up what sociologists – and now government – refer to as 'social capital'.

Social capital

The term 'social capital' draws attention to the fact that the ability of individuals to make a difference to their environments and lives is immeasurably enhanced if they can act in concert with other individuals and not on their own. In order for that to happen there needs to be frequent informal and formal contact between people in each group and locality. As a result, people develop their capacity for sympathy and goodwill and see what needs to be done to help their neighbour and improve their environment. This is social capital.

The idea of social capital has been understood for at least the last 100 years. L. J. Hanifan, an American, was probably the first to use the term, writing in 1916 that continuous contact with one's neighbour, and the neighbour with others, brings

> ... an accumulation of social capital, which may immediately satisfy his social needs and which may bear a social potentiality sufficient to the substantial improvement of living conditions in the whole community. The community as a whole will benefit by the cooperation of all its parts, while the individual will find in his associations the advantages of the help, sympathy, and the fellowship of his neighbours.[2]

However, it was not until neighbourhood and other groups began to decline in the second half of the last century that the term was rediscovered and entered the popular sociological lexicon.

There are various forms of social capital but a useful distinction can be made between two major types: 'bonding' or 'inward-looking'; and 'bridging' or 'outward-looking'. The Dorothy Road Fellowship was essentially an example of bonding social capital: it looked inwards to its own members. It had an exclusive membership – only people who lived in the street qualified, and it was for their exclusive benefit. It scarcely ever raised issues that concerned anyone other than those in the Fellowship – though there was a collection for east-coast flood victims in 1953, probably because this was a part of the world we all knew well from summer holidays: Leicester's industry closed down every August and workers and their families resumed relationships again for two weeks in Skegness or Mablethorpe. As we have seen, this type of social capital bonds people together in tightly drawn networks of support. Bonding social capital works for the benefit of the whole group, though in so doing gives additional particular satisfactions for individuals as well. The Dorothy Road Fellowship provided entertainment for all the children of the street at parties and outings throughout the year, but it also thereby enabled those who enjoyed putting on Punch and Judy shows or got a kick out of catering or organizing events, or just liked children, to satisfy some of their own individual emotional needs and ambitions. Sometimes the Fellowship could play quite a critical role in individuals' lives, since through the network of relationships people learnt about job opportunities or who might be interested in sharing childcare arrangements.

The second type of social capital is 'bridging' social capital, where groups look outwards and build bridges with other groups within the wider community. When I returned to Leicester in the late 1960s for my first job as a curate, I joined two groups that were examples of bridging social capital: an ecumenical group that brought together people from all the main Christian denominations; and a group formed to combat racism that embraced like-minded people from across the ethnic, political and religious spectrum. Membership of both these groups was of great importance to me. It broadened not just my knowledge of people different from me but my understanding and sympathy towards them. Churches can be examples of one or both types of social capital. A church that is exclusive and inward-looking – such as the Jehovah's Witnesses – is one thing;[3] a church that bonds its members together but also builds bridges to the wider community, and perhaps the world, is another. (One way of distinguishing congregations in a way that is more illuminating than a simple denominational category is to undertake a 'bonding and bridging' test.)

Sometimes sociologists will speak of a third type of social capital, namely 'linking capital';[4] but this is a type of bridging capital and refers to the capacity of a group of people to make links with powerful organizations beyond the locality – such as the local authority, the strategic partnership, the housing association – and to exert influence there. As individuals we often feel powerless before bureaucracies whether local or national. Being part of an organized group brings strength – the capacity to challenge or confront.

We could say, therefore, that a cohesive community is one in which both bonding and bridging social capital is being built. When the government speaks about 'integration' – rather than assimilation or parallel lives – and not just cohesion, bridging capital is essentially what they are pointing to. They want the different ethnic, cultural and faith groups that make up a given community to get to know one another.

All social groups build social capital. The middle classes understand very well the value of social capital, which they acquire through extensive networking – from dinner parties and the golf club to casual contacts in the supermarket car park or at the school fund-raising barbecue.

The decline of social capital

At some point in the late 1960s, the Dorothy Road Fellowship was wound up. It had been struggling for many years, failing to recruit younger members or to attract people in any numbers to its social programmes – old-time dancing, bingo (called 'housey-housey') and whist drives. The blame for the collapse was variously attributed to aspects of modern life – television, greater prosperity, busier working lives – and sometimes to a growth of antisocial vices – greater individualism and selfishness. There was no doubt some truth in all of this, but the greatest impact on the working-class area in which I lived was first the slum clearance programme that demolished some of the poorer homes and removed the population to outlying council estates, and then the arrival during the 1960s of an Asian immigrant population that found the small terraced houses of the inner city attractive to rent and later to buy. They tended to keep themselves to themselves: the women did not speak English and were not encouraged to socialize; the men worked shifts and long hours; they looked to their own organizations to satisfy religious and social needs. They did not join the Fellowship and I doubt whether the Fellowship would have encouraged them anyway. When I was a teenager my family followed many others and became part of the 'white flight' to outer estates in the suburbs. The rising prosperity of these years, together with my parents' frugality, enabled us to move from rented property and buy a small, semi-detached house. We became part of the statistics that show that home ownership jumped from 26 per cent in 1945 to 53 per cent in 1976.[5] But one effect of the move to the suburbs was to make us more family-centred and less outward-looking; we knew little or nothing of our new neighbours.[6] Even so, my parents had left indelibly fixed in my young mind the idea that responsible citizens took an interest in their localities and had obligations towards their neighbours.

The demise of the Dorothy Road Fellowship was part of a wider pattern. The evidence suggests that for several decades there has been a widespread and overall decline in de Tocqueville's 'little platoons' across all social groups, and therefore a loss of social capital.[7] In 2007, the Royal Society for the Encouragement of Arts, Manufactures and Commerce (RSA) published a report based on a YouGov poll that found that increasing numbers of Britons from all social classes did not join or support voluntary societies. Membership of organizations as diverse as the Women's Institute, the Boy Scouts, trade unions and political parties had all fallen dramatically. This led one Sunday newspaper to headline its report of the RSA's findings: 'The rise of can't-be-bothered Britain'.[8]

The same pattern of decline in civic engagement had been detected in the USA. Robert Putnam charted it in his book, *Bowling Alone*, and attempted to quantify the contribution that various factors have made to the falling away. He attributes the decline to the following:

- Pressures of time and money, including both parents being at work – 10 per cent.
- The move to the suburbs and greater commuting – 10 per cent.
- Electronic entertainment and the privatization of leisure, especially due to television – 25 per cent.
- Generational change as the civic generation was replaced by their children and grandchildren – 50 per cent.

There is some overlap of the categories and Putnam also acknowledges that there is a significant gap in current knowledge about the causes, which is why the percentages fall short of 100.[9] What this suggests, however, is a loss of social capital, with considerable implications for community cohesion.

The relative resilience of religion

When my family left the inner city for the suburbs in the later 1950s, the focus of our concerns turned more inwards – as it did with others who made the same journey – from the wider neighbourhood to the family, though with one exception: we transferred to a new church. The churches have proved to be among the more resilient of voluntary groups, even though they too have declined substantially in the post-war years. The extent of the decline – an aspect of secularization – and the reasons for it are the subject of ongoing debate among sociologists and historians, with little consensus. However, there are some areas of agreement. For example, almost all would accept that in the period immediately after the war the churches enjoyed growth in attendance, while at some point towards the end of the 1950s and over the next decade there was a fall that has continued to the present time.[10] Steve Bruce argues that this represents a much longer trajectory of decline dating back at least to the Reformation. Moreover, this decline now looks terminal, not least because the Church is failing to replicate itself – the children of the immediate post-war generations who were churchgoers are not attending.[11] Callum Brown believes the beginning of the collapse of Christianity can be firmly dated from the 1960s and is principally the result of younger women leaving in large numbers.[12] This had a number of far-reaching additional consequences. As the women left, their male partners tended to follow them. Most critical of all, the women who left did not raise their children in the faith. Generational changes seem to have been at least as important as any other factor. For Brown, as for Bruce, the decline is terminal if not almost complete. Brown ends his book by saying, 'Britain is showing the world how religion as we have known it can die.'[13]

The advent of other religions has also had an effect. There has been a small trickle of conversions – though they have gone in both directions.[14] But more significant is the way the presence of other faiths along the high street has had a relativizing effect. The way we have dealt with religious pluralism – in schools, for example – is by not privileging any one faith. So whereas when I was at school, Christianity was taught as true (and by implication other faiths were not true), now all faiths have to be considered on a par, and the easiest way of doing that is to think of religion as a matter of subjective belief – 'true' for me though not necessarily 'true' for anyone else – and to take a comparative-religions approach. But something that is 'true for me but not for you' is something that resembles opinion rather than truth.[15] The RE teacher has been the unwitting agent of a relativizing tendency that has probably done more to undermine religion than the most aggressive atheism. It leads not to a reasoned opposition but to an unreasoning indifference.

But while all can agree that something of significance began to happen to organized religion in the middle years of the last century, not all see the undoubted decline as either total or irreversible. The overall figures, in any case, mask other changes. So, for example, it seems that while the more mainstream and liberal churches have suffered losses, more conservative and charismatic churches – evangelical and Pentecostal – have been growing in numbers and 'planting' new congregations.[16] There is growth and decline, even though the aggregate figures show loss.[17] The growing congregations of whatever denomination share similar characteristics.[18] They tend to be 'harder edged', having clearer boundaries for membership than the more liberal churches. They also have an emphasis on teaching and preaching – with conviction and certainty – rather than social concerns. They appeal to emotion as much as reason, the heart as well as the head.[19] Moreover, the growing congregations seem more successful in retaining the allegiance of their children. If present trends continue, eventually evangelical congregations will become the majority as well as the most vibrant.

The pattern of church attendance also seems to have changed. Whereas my parents' generation were weekly worshippers, more recent generations have become more occasional attenders – though evangelicals are more likely to be weekly. This means that figures for Sunday attendance alone now need careful interpretation. If people are attending less frequently, which in itself may or may not be a measure of secularization, the numbers for any one Sunday would not be a reliable guide to the overall numbers of those who regularly participate in worship. The Sunday attendance figures are currently at around 6–7 per cent, which probably means that 9–10 per cent of the population attend church at some point during the month. But the figure is considerably more at the major festivals, especially Christmas. These percentages translate into around one million regular worshippers for each of the major denominational groups – Anglicans, Roman Catholics and Free Churches. These are significant numbers and are perhaps one reason why there is no great appetite to see religion removed altogether from public life. The Church of England remains established with the monarch as Supreme Governor and 26 of its bishops in the House of Lords.

But the picture needs filling out a little further. In 2001, the national census asked people to give their religion – or to say they had no religion. The question was not a compulsory part of the census though in the event most people completed this section. The

Table 1 Census 2001 – percentages of the population of Great Britain by religion	
Christian	71.8
Muslim	2.8
Hindu	1.0
Sikh	0.6
Jewish	0.5
Buddhist	0.3
Other religion	0.3
No religion	15.1
Not stated	7.8
(Total non-Christian 5.4)	

Table 2 Census 2001 – percentages of the non-Christian religious population	
Muslim	51.9
Hindu	18.3
Sikh	11.0
Jewish	8.7
Buddhist	4.9
Other religion	5.2

results were that 76.8 per cent of the population of the UK declared themselves as having a religious 'affiliation' (see Tables 1 and 2): 71.8 per cent Christian; 2.8 per cent Muslim; 1 per cent Hindu; 0.6 per cent Sikh; 0.5 per cent Jewish; 0.3 per cent Buddhist; and 0.3 per cent other religions. It is far from obvious how these statistics are to be understood. It is possible, for example, that because the questions asked about religion were near to those asked about race, some people called themselves 'Christian' to mean 'white' as opposed to 'Muslim' and 'Asian'. It is equally possible that many define the various religious categories in a wider cultural sense. At any rate, there does seem to be a large section of the British people who may not be regular churchgoers but who do want to identify with religion in some way. This is perhaps why a further aspect of religion in Britain today, hard to capture in purely statistical terms, needs to be noted, namely the persistence of the so-called occasional offices and pastoral services.

The occasional offices of the church are those services that mark important moments in the life cycle – births, marriages and deaths – christenings (infant baptisms), weddings and funerals. Although there has been a fall here as well, significant numbers of people continue to bring children for baptism and to be married in churches, while the overwhelming majority of funerals are according to a religious rite. It seems that at key moments in people's lives, religious rites are still widely sought. I call this phenomenon leading secular lives while retaining sacred hearts, and have written about it more extensively elsewhere.[20]

It is also noticeable how churches are able to play important roles as focuses for the emotions of communities and sometimes of the nation as a whole when tragedy strikes. When, for example, two young girls, Jessica Chapman and Holly Wells, went missing and were subsequently found murdered in Soham, Cambridgeshire, in August 2002, the community's anxiety then grief was focused on the Anglican parish church. The Rector, the Revd Tim Alban Jones, encouraged people to visit the church and churchyard to lay flowers, light candles and say prayers. He skilfully managed a great deal of the community's shock, grief and anger through carefully arranged liturgies and acts of worship and remembrance. Five years before this the Dean and chapter of Westminster Abbey constructed a liturgy for the funeral of Princess Diana that seemed able to touch large numbers of people across the country and even across the world. It is hard to see what other organization could have performed such a task. As long as the national church can do this, it will remain 'established' in the life of the nation and each local community, whatever its constitutional status.[21] Another way of expressing this is to say that while the Anglican Church continues to fulfil these needs, it can continue to make a case for constitutional establishment.

All of this has led one sociologist, Grace Davie, to characterize British Christianity as 'believing without belonging' and to speak of 'vicarious' Christianity. In other words, although many continue to believe in the main tenets of the Christian faith, they do not want to become regular churchgoers or perhaps churchgoers at all, but are very glad to have others do their churchgoing for them and for the Church to be there for the rites of passage.[22]

What we can say, therefore, is that the majority of people in the UK remain influenced by religion, particularly Christianity, though they do not want to be greatly involved with organized religion and rarely attend places of worship. They seem happy enough to call themselves Christian and to have the loose form of establishment that is represented by the monarch as supreme head of the Church of England, as long as there is sensitivity towards those who belong to other denominations or other religions – or have no religion at all. In that spirit and with that understanding they are supportive of chaplaincies in prisons, hospitals and the armed forces. They will even have affection for 'Thought for the Day' each morning at breakfast-time on BBC Radio 4. The Queen captured this diversity very well in her inclusive Christmas address, quoted at the head of this chapter.

Even so, the number of people saying they have no religion has been rising steadily since the 1950s, reaching 15.1 per cent according to the 2001 national census. This has led to a change in the general attitude of society towards religion, not least to the way religion is dealt with in the media. One shrewd observer, the historian Hugh McLeod, has noted that in more recent years 'those who rejected Christianity were increasingly ready to say so loudly and openly'.[23] In the 1950s, if public figures were anti-religious they would probably consider it prudent not to say so. But by 2007, not only were there many prominent journalists and writers who frequently wrote against religion – Polly Toynbee in the *Guardian*, Matthew Parris in *The Times*, the novelists Philip Pullman and Martin Amis – but the leader of the Liberal Democrats, Nick Clegg, felt able to declare himself an atheist, something unthinkable only a few decades earlier for any party leader, let alone of the party of the nonconformist conscience. Even so, some would argue that the increasing attacks on religion are themselves a backhanded acknowledgement that religion is still a force to be reckoned with in the contemporary world. Why else bother with it? As John Gray has written, 'secularization is in retreat, and the result is the appearance of an evangelical type of atheism not see since Victorian times'.[24]

Religious groups and social capital

But if churches are in overall decline and the critics of religion are more vocal, why has government shown renewed interest in religious groups over the past decade or so? The answer is twofold. On the one hand, the government has become concerned about the apparent disaffection of some among the minority ethnic communities following the disturbances of 2001, and recognizes that for many from those communities, religion is an important part of their life and identity. Attendance at places of worship for them is at a relatively high level, so they can be engaged through their religious organizations. On the other hand, as the government contemplated the decline of civic engagement with growing anxiety, it noted the way religious congregations were often more tenacious and capable of surviving than many other groups. For all their weaknesses, Christian churches continue to be a significant presence in both rural and urban areas. Tom Butler, the Bishop of Southwark, has said that while 'local faith communities often feel themselves to be fragile and weak, yet the truth is that they are often the strongest local community groupings and certainly the most comprehensive'.[25] They can be like a tree in whose branches many birds find a place to settle.

One of the strengths of the Church of England, for example, is its ubiquity. The church is organized on a territorial basis with dioceses and parishes, which means that, however thin, it has a presence in almost every part of the country. In some rural areas, while the school, the pub, the post office and even the village hall may have closed, the parish church has often remained; in some urban areas, the church may be one of the few genuinely local groups remaining. Put briefly, the government sees religion as a source of social capital that cannot be ignored. It also sees faith groups as a potential partner 'on the ground' locally. Writing in 2004, the Home Secretary, David Blunkett, spoke of 'the growing record of partnership between public agencies and faith communities in the delivery of services'.[26] For instance, churches and church members are often at the forefront of neighbourhood renewal schemes and involved with Urban Regeneration Companies, Local Strategic Partnerships and Regional Development Agencies.

The more traditional and mainstream churches have always had both an inward and an outward focus – examples of 'bonding' and 'bridging' social capital. They have taught their members not just to have regard to their own spiritual lives and the life of their church but also to be concerned for the wider community and its needs – and the world. We can see a good, historic example of this encouragement in the Litany of the Church of England. The Litany is a form of responsorial prayer that would have been used in every Anglican parish several times a year if not weekly for 400 years. It is a wonderful exercise in practical and everyday charity:

> That it may please thee to succour, help and comfort, all that are in danger, necessity and tribulation . . .
> that it may please thee to defend, and provide for, the fatherless and widows, and all that are desolate and oppressed . . .

that it may please thee to have mercy on all men . . .
We beseech thee to hear us, good Lord.

The sentiments expressed here have provided the ethical basis for many crucial social movements in British history, including the abolition of slavery, prison and factory reform and the care of orphans.[27] Church members continue to support over 23,000 religious-based charities in England and Wales today.[28]

The mainstream churches, standing in this tradition, encourage outside bodies to meet on their premises. If I look at those groups meeting in the last church for which I was responsible as parish priest, St George's Church, Kendal, these are the groups that met regularly in 2007: Alcoholics Anonymous; Rainbows (junior Brownies); St George's Players (a drama group); the Amabile Girls' Choir; Kendal Judo Club; Line-dancing Group; the Mothers' Union; the Church Fellowship (older members of the parish); St George's Men's Group; Church Singers; Friday Night Youth Club; Marks & Spencer's pensioners group; and the management committee of a local children's home. In other words, the church building enabled a significant number of Kendal's 'little platoons' to exist. Some bigger congregations will have even more extensive social and recreational programmes.

One very important development of that tradition in the second half of the twentieth century was the creation of the Church Urban Fund in response to the publication of *Faith in the City* in 1985.[29] Over the years the Fund has raised more than £60 million from church members to finance over 5,000 local projects in the poorest 10 per cent of urban priority areas.[30] It is currently committed to spending £3 million per annum.

Churches do more than make their buildings available for others to use. Individual church members are often significantly involved in secular organizations as well as their church.[31] The government's Citizenship Survey of 2005 found that 52 per cent of the religiously observant participated in some form of civic involvement.[32] Again, if I think about my last congregation and the other groups they engaged with, both locally and nationally, the list is impressive for a congregation of just over 100 in a small market town. Members were involved, often at committee, trustee or board level, with: Voluntary Service Overseas; the Youth Justice Board for England and

Wales; the Royal College of Nursing; the Freemasons; Lions Clubs International; Probus; the Full Gospel Businessmen's Fellowship; the Westmorland General Hospital League of Friends; Springfield House Women's Hostel; the Kendal Photographic Society; the Civic Society; the Francis Scott Charitable Trust; the University of the Third Age; Staveley Amateur Operatic Society; Kendal and District Gilbert and Sullivan Society; Cubs, Scouts and Sea Cadets; the Young Farmers Club; the Conservative Party; the Labour Party; the Christian Socialist Movement; the Liberal Democrats; the local council; the magistracy; Neighbourhood Watch; the British Legion; school governors; meals on wheels; prison visitors; two local choirs – and so on. They were also heavily involved in various campaigning groups, such as Amnesty International and Make Poverty History. In short, church members play critical roles in the entirety of civic life and not simply as members of a faith group. In inner-city areas this may be even more the case. In recent years, for instance, many clergy have found themselves at the forefront of ambitious community development, regeneration and neighbourhood renewal schemes.

We should not, of course, overestimate either the strength or the capacity of the British churches. They play an important social role but they are nowhere near as important in this respect as churches in the USA where, some would argue, they are the 'single most important repository of social capital'.[33] America is one of the most religiously observant countries in the developed world, and the churches often run extensive educational, recreational and social service programmes, as well as services and prayer groups. Unlike Europe, as it industrialized and urbanized, America became a more not a less religiously committed country, formal church membership rising from 17 per cent in 1776 to 62 per cent in 1980.[34] In England and Wales, even in a more religious age – the nineteenth century – churchgoing probably never exceeded 40 per cent.[35] Even so, comparable to churches there are few other organizations meeting in every part of the country on a weekly basis.

Other faith communities

But perhaps of even greater significance for inner urban areas has been the growing confidence shown by the minority faiths.[36] When my family left inner-city Leicester for an outer estate, mosques and temples were few in number and members of minority faiths often met in secular premises. There was little engagement with other religious or secular groups, and the non-Asian community, white and black, tended to be wary if not hostile. By the beginning of the present century, domes and minarets were on almost every urban skyline, and most major urban centres had purpose-built mosques, gurdwaras and temples. In what follows I will speak about Muslims, but many of the points will apply to other faith communities as well.

Faith-based organizations are of the utmost importance in developing social capital among the UK's minority ethnic groups, which according to the 2001 census make up 7.9 per cent of the UK population, about 4.6 million people. The point here is that the only people who can organize and administer the local mosque are the members of the local faith community themselves, who are overwhelmingly members of the ethnic minorities. In this respect, these places of worship in inner-city areas are playing a role with regard to ethnic minorities that is analogous to the role the Methodist societies played for the white working and lower middle classes of the eighteenth and nineteenth centuries. Aspirant working- and lower-middle-class men and women found their ambition to play a role in the Anglican Church (and the parochial organizations connected with it) simply thwarted – the national church did not encourage ambition but rather taught the virtue of knowing one's place. Every Anglican boy and girl would learn the Catechism, a way of teaching the faith by rote learning: the curate of the parish would recite a series of questions and the children would chorus the answer. The section concerned with social ethics was this:

Question   What is thy duty towards thy neighbour?

Answer   My duty towards my Neighbour, is to love him as myself, and to do to all men, as I would they should do unto me: To love, honour, and succour my father and mother: To honour and obey the Queen, and all that are put in authority under her: To submit myself to all my governors, teachers, spiritual pastors and masters: To order myself lowly and reverently to all my betters: To hurt no body by word nor deed: To be true and just in all my dealing: To bear no malice nor hatred in my heart: To keep my hands from picking and stealing, and my tongue from evilspeaking, lying, and slandering: To keep my body in temperance, soberness, and chastity: Not to covet nor desire other men's goods; but to learn and labour truly to get mine own living, and to do my duty in that state of life, unto which it shall please God to call me.[37]

'To do my duty in that state of life, unto which it shall please God to call me', was essentially a way of maintaining the status quo in church and state. It did little to encourage anyone to have opinions of their own or aspire to leadership or economic and social betterment. Leadership remained firmly in the hands of those who were always of a different and superior social standing. So the Methodists, while at first remaining members of the Church of England, increasingly began to organize themselves in separate societies, and eventually as a separate church, where working-class and lower-middle-class men and women could administer their own affairs, organize worship and charity, and preach. In short, Methodism put religion into the hands of ordinary people and ordinary people responded by forsaking the Church of England for Methodism.

After the war, the immigrant Afro-Caribbean community, being mainly Christian, at first sought to be part of existing churches, including the Methodists. But when they were denied the possibility of influencing worship or being part of the leadership, local or national, they soon removed themselves and formed their own churches. A wheel came full circle, for just as working people left the Church of England in the eighteenth century to form their own Methodist churches, so Afro-Caribbean people gave up on white Methodism in the twentieth and set up Pentecostal churches. These churches have enabled many individuals to acquire in the religious arena important social skills that are transferable to other contexts – an ability to plan and organize, a confidence to speak before a large gathering of people. They have also brought spiritual healing to lives that would otherwise be broken under life's disappointments and rebuffs.

In the same way, the appearance of purpose-built mosques marked the growing self-confidence of minority faiths in organizing their own affairs. It also meant that liberal society had to deal with them differently. One of the temptations of liberals in positions of power is to treat members of ethnic minorities as victims. This enables the liberal to remain in a position of dominance while appearing sympathetic. (This is exactly what liberation theology in Latin America amounts to, for liberation theology crucially needs theologians to explain how analysis and exegesis works.) At first, minority faith groups accepted that victim role – but no more. Increasingly they engage or want to engage as equals and to make a contribution – though the debilitating language of victimhood is not completely dead and some among the ethnic minorities have made a career out of exploiting it. The mosques provide support as people learn the skills they need to act confidently in modern society – exactly as the Methodist Church once did for working men and women in the eighteenth and nineteenth centuries. As Rumman Ahmed has written, membership of a mosque also brings with it being part of 'vital personal support networks'.[38]

The sacred marinade

Faith groups, then, are a key resource for community cohesion – hence the government's interest in them. Even the most ardent secularist would recognize that they can make invaluable contributions towards the creation of social capital. We could list some of these contributions in this way (while recognizing that they are not the only groups meeting in an area and encouraging forms of life conducive to cohesion):

- Faith brings people together and so builds 'bonding social capital' in particular localities or among particular ethnic/religious groups; it builds trust between people of different cultures and ethnicities.
- Traditional religion (of all faiths) encourages members to spend time with their families, to be good husbands and wives, diligent workers, loving parents and respectful children.
- Each faith community has traditions of reflecting on and propagating the virtues and values needed for healthy communities that are embedded in their traditions – concern for the neighbour, hospitality, civility, honest dealing, truth-telling, peace-keeping.
- Members of faith communities tend to know a large number of people in their locality by virtue of their membership ('social connectivity'), which strengthens 'bridging' social capital.
- They generally encourage members to be active citizens by urging them to use their vote and promote the welfare of their fellow citizens through volunteering or charitable giving.[39]

- They involve individuals meeting together regularly to exchange ideas and information and can give people a critical perspective on issues affecting their neighbourhood.
- They are usually committed to localities for long periods of time and have a concern for people's long-term and not merely short-term interests.
- Sometimes, the priest or minister may well be the only professionally trained person living in a socially deprived area, where they can offer leadership.
- They may offer a channel to some of the hardest-to-reach groups.[40]
- The horizons and sympathies of members may be broadened through links with other countries – through missionary societies, aid agencies or, in the case of ethnic minorities, through family connections.

In all of this, the contribution of the faith group to the well-being of its local community can be out of all proportion to the size of the group.[41]

We could probably also argue, more controversially, that religion contributes towards a law-abiding society. Professor Christie Davies, a sociologist at Reading University, believes there is a strong correlation between rates of crime in the UK and degrees of religious observance. The nation was at its most law-abiding when children were sent to Sunday School in high numbers.[42] In the first decades of the twentieth century, half the nation's children under 15 were enrolled, and even as late as 1957 three-quarters of the over-30s had been through Sunday School. Yet by the end of the century the figure was less than 10 per cent. The influence that the teaching and examples imparted here have on young minds can scarcely be exaggerated, and yet it is so easily overlooked. 'An entire culture', Davies writes, 'had been lost.' At the same time the crime figures rose, especially after 1955 – the time when church attendances began to fall dramatically following a small upward movement after the war. In 1957, around 500,000 notifiable offences were recorded; by 1997 this had risen to 4,500,000. The prison population likewise rose from 10,500 in 1937 (only 800 prisoners serving sentences of more than three years) to 64,000 in 1997 (23,000 on longer sentences) and over 80,000 by 2007.

We could also chart the gradual collapse of the temperance movement – closely associated with Protestant churches – over this same
period, and the rise of excessive drinking, especially among young
people. In some towns and villages, many would see the greatest
threat to community cohesion coming from alcohol-fuelled young
people. And as well as alcohol there is now a serious drug problem.
In 1953, 290 addicts were known to the Home Office; by the end of
the century, 20,000 heroin users were registered.[43]

This is not to make a case for religious observance on utilitarian
grounds. Even if these correlations are correct, or even if a stronger
causal connection could be established, no one is going to turn to
religious faith for these reasons. But it is to draw attention to the
cultural factors, including religious commitment, that bear on community cohesion. It is also to suggest that the decline of religion that
many secularists work hard to achieve may have consequences for
community life that we shall all come to regret.

The religious future

But what of the religious future? Projecting anything as unpredict-
able as religious faith is hazardous. In the nineteenth and early part
of the twentieth century many, with varying mixtures of relish or
regret, predicted the gradual withering away of religion – Marx,
Freud, Durkheim. Religion could express fine and noble sentiments – the heart of a heartless world – or be the glue that held
society together; but it would not long survive the advent of the
modern age with its rational, scientific approach, its technological
mastery of the natural world and its pluralism. In the event, organized religion has proved more resilient, though less so in Europe than
in the USA and the rest of the world. But what does seem possible
is that if attrition of the British Christian community continues at
the present rate, and if the birth rate among ethnic minorities holds
up and they continue to retain their young people in the faith, the
landscape of organized religion in the UK will look very different well
before the end of the twenty-first century. For while Christianity
struggles, Islam is enjoying something of a resurgence.

As we look to the future of religion we can detect some trends
and new developments that could militate against the building of
social capital and so community cohesion. The first concerns trends

within the Christian churches; the other possible trends within other faiths, particularly Islam.

Growth of evangelicalism

First, we have seen that while the number of observant Christians is falling overall, there are growing as well as declining churches, and the growing churches are evangelical and Pentecostal. But these congregations have by and large not always shown the same social concern as the more mainstream churches.[44] Their focus has tended to be inward rather than outward, creating bonding rather than bridging social capital. Their highly committed members are more likely to spend time in church groups than in secular groups. Their church polity is 'associational' rather than community – which is to say that they do not attend the parish church or the nearest church because it is local, but seek out an evangelical or Pentecostal church of their choice, which may be a considerable distance away. As a result, these associational congregations do not necessarily have any particular interest in or affinity with or affection for the neighbourhood in which they happen to be set.

Evangelical Christians work with a world and faith dualism that can make them guarded and suspicious about a great deal of secular activity. As a result, they have a tendency to create their own Christian organizations to meet specific needs, rather than engage with or join secular organizations: evangelical groups exist for teachers, doctors, counsellors – even motor cyclists. Even when they have an interest in secular issues – such as global warming or poverty in the developing world – they tend to debate the issues among themselves, often producing excellent materials for discussion, rather than join with others. They may even be suspicious of more liberal Christians. This is because more liberal forms of Christianity seem to them to be a weakening of the faith: they do not present the Christian message with clarity or certainty. As a consequence, they believe liberal Christians run the risk of being more influenced by the secular culture than the other way round. Evangelical Christians are often reluctant to engage in ecumenical dialogue, and regard interfaith activities with considerable caution if not downright opposition.

At the heart of evangelical Christianity are narratives of transformation and transfiguration. The message is about a wicked and

fallen world from which men and women can be saved and re-
deemed and lives turned around. This is why in many evangelical
churches personal testimony plays an important part at some point.
Testimonies are cameo spiritual biographies, telling how a particular individual's life was transformed by the intervention of the Holy
Spirit. They can be very powerful instruments of evangelism precisely
because they are the authentic and sincere account of the individual
concerned. Testimonies may be given by lay members at Sunday services or at special events or on the occasion of someone's baptism.[45]
This inevitably leads to distinctions being drawn between the saved
and the unsaved. The tendency then is to see the world simply as a
mission-field of the unsaved. Even when ministry and programmes
of pastoral care face outwards, they are undertaken because they
provide opportunities for further evangelism and conversion.

It also follows from this that the reformation of society depends
on and follows from the reformation of individuals within society.
The most important transformations will not come about by direct
action in the world – politics – but indirectly by changing individuals. Much of the government's language of community empowerment will jar with evangelicals. For them empowerment comes from
a spiritual not a secular source. Indeed, government discourse will
more than jar: it will seem absurd, because evangelicals know that if
a community is to turn around the lives of feckless husbands and neg-
ligent mothers, or selfish entrepreneurs and exploitative employers,
it needs a spiritual revolution, not a new government initiative.

But in more recent years evangelicals have been challenged to
turn outwards in order to be of service and not simply to win
further converts. For example, Holy Trinity Brompton, the leading
Anglican evangelical church and centre of the Alpha movement, has
a well-developed social engagement programme that is distinct from
its evangelizing activities. If that trend continues, it would be a significant development, for these groups are empowered by their faith,
not easily deterred and are capable of considerable acts of altruism,
generosity and sacrifice if they believe this is Christ's will.

If the future vitality of Christianity in the UK lies primarily with
evangelicals, they need to be encouraged to engage and form partnerships with non-Christian and secular groups if the impact of
Christianity on society overall is not to diminish further. It is hard
to know whether this lack of engagement on the part of evangelicals

reflects the general loss of confidence in the face of growing secularization experienced across all denominations, or whether it is based on some theological objection. It may be an unresolved mix of the two. The challenge to those evangelical leaders who understand the need for engagement is for them to help the rest of their members recognize it as well. It is this wider social role that twentieth-century evangelical Christians – unlike their eighteenth- and nineteenth-century forbears – were generally unwilling to undertake.

Privatization of religion

The second trend in religion that may not contribute much, if anything, to social capital is its growing 'privatization'. 'Spirituality' is being cut loose from its anchorage in buildings, liturgies and organized religion and is more 'free floating'. There is evidence that this trend poses a serious threat to more traditional building-based and organized faith. In 2000, researchers from Lancaster University's Religious Studies Department undertook one of the biggest programmes of research into religious observance and practice in the UK.[46] The project centred on Kendal in Cumbria and involved research that was both quantitative (measuring and counting) and qualitative (listening and asking). The researchers found that even in this fairly traditional English market town, churchgoing was more or less in line with the national average – at about 7 per cent. They also found a growing number of alternative spiritual practices (53 in Kendal), such as yoga, shiatsu, reiki, wild-women group, circle dancing and psychic consultancy. Those engaged in these alternatives were often hostile to more traditional organized forms of religion. The claim of the researchers was that these newer forms of spirituality are growing whereas organized religion looks tired and is shrinking, and that within a couple of decades or so there will be more practitioners of alternative spiritualities than of organized religions.

In fact there have always been forms of working-class spirituality that have existed 'below the radar' of religious sociologists – something that seems to have escaped the notice of the researchers. When I was a small child there would be a regular queue of people – mainly women – at my grandmother's house: she was an accomplished reader of tea leaves (up to the invention of the tea bag), though they also came for the tea and a good gossip. And my aunt was a type of spiritualist and do-it-yourself astrologer. While many of these working-class practices have vanished, there is a growth of more middle-class person-centred spiritualities that can be practised either by individuals on their own or in small groups. But they do not necessarily result in any long-term commitment to the group or the building of much social capital.

What we are describing here is what has been called the 'expressive revolution' and 'expressive individualism' – of which the Queen was very aware when she made the remarks in her Christmas broadcast quoted above. The origins of this cultural shift lie in the Romantic movement of the late eighteenth century,[47] for our purposes an attempt, mainly by intellectuals, to find more authentic ways of living and expressing themselves.

What seems to have happened more recently is that this has become a mass phenomenon. We can see the evidence in the book-shops along every high street: self-help manuals explaining various techniques whereby the individual can be put in touch with his or her 'real' self, many suggesting that organized religion, far from being the answer to someone's spiritual hunger, is actually the prob-lem. The argument about organized religion runs like this: you have to fit its predetermined ideas about your spiritual condition (usually that you are a sinner) and subscribe to its remedies (prayer, confession, the sacrament); the new approach allows you to explore and discover – you are not forced into a mould of someone else's making, however venerable. What is essential is that you choose a particular spiritual practice and do so on the basis that it speaks to you, it empowers you in your spiritual life and your life more generally. Truth in religion is what works for you.

It goes without saying that spirituality of this kind is inevitably and unlimitedly plural. The watchwords, therefore, are 'authenticity', 'sincerity', 'exploration', 'freedom', 'choice'. Hate-words would in-clude 'authority' and 'sin', the latter being especially suspect: people must be free to explore, including exploring their dark or shadow side, and make mistakes for themselves – all of which the church calls sin.

It can sound selfish, but it would be a mistake to think that those who are part of the expressive revolution are only interested in themselves and their own spiritual needs. They are often keenly motivated to live lives that respect the natural world and have a concern for the world's poor. Authenticity, Oxfam and green politics seem to go hand in hand.

Part of the expressive revolution is the sexual revolution of the twentieth century. Among intellectuals and the upper classes this began before the Second World War. They increasingly felt able to speak openly about their sexuality and admit publicly to being homosexual or bisexual. But it was not until the late 1960s that people across all social classes felt increasingly able to 'be them-selves'. (Even so, we would have to acknowledge that it is still diffi-cult for working-class men to admit to being gay. Some professional footballers have had a very hostile reception from crowds after they have 'come out' or been 'outed'.)

Enough has been said to indicate why the expressive revolution has been seen as a threat to organized religion, not least by the clergy. For the present the effects of this have been felt principally among Christians. To some extent, the newer, more charismatic forms of evangelicalism are a response to this since they too encourage people to express themselves emotionally in worship – within, of course, the traditional understanding of orthodox Christianity. Much will depend on how far traditional churches allow their mem-bers to adapt. But who can predict what the consequences will be for other faiths?

Enclavization

The third development in religion that may not contribute towards community cohesion or, more broadly, social (that is, national) cohesion is the desire or tendency on the part of some among minority faith communities, though especially the Muslim com-munity, to remain firmly within their own communities and not seek further engagement with other groups, secular or religious. It is, of course, a mistake to think that the Muslim community is mono-lithic or reacts in a uniform way. For example, there are mosques, such as those of the Deoband tradition, that are conservative, set-ting great store by preserving the community and its traditions from corrupting Western influence; there are teachers who emphasize personal spiritual transformation and renewal, such as those within Tablighi Jama'at; there are modernists who happily embrace an agenda of accommodation with modernity;[48] there are Islamists who preach a political version of Islam and want political power only ever in the hands of people like themselves – they regard many fellow Muslims, as well as non-Muslims, as infidels.[49] All of these vie with one another within the Muslim community.

The majority of Muslims in the UK are from South Asia, and the majority of those are from Pakistan. On the whole, they are not from the poorest and most rural parts of Pakistan but those areas that have a long tradition of migration in search of a better life.[50] As far as community cohesion goes, much may now depend on how far the Muslim community will choose to remain in its urban enclaves and how far it will follow the path of many previous migrant groups and with greater prosperity become more diffuse within the wider population by making the traditional British journey from the inner city to the suburbs, from the suburbs to the market towns and rural villages. For the moment, the Muslim communities in towns like Burnley and Bradford remain close-knit communities that form something like urban villages, with their own 'socially, linguistically and ethnically defined borders... interacting in a selective way with the broader society around'.[51] The demand for Sharia courts and Sharia law to be recognized may be one sign of this. But in so far as there are global pressures within Islam to become more conservative, the end result may be less, not more, engagement with other faith groups and with the wider society.

A particular problem is that of the second generation of immigrants, those younger people who were born in the UK yet whose families have strong links with other parts of the world. At some point, as they work through the question of identity and multiple identity – which is common to all young people now – they have to deal especially with the issue of what it is to be both British and also in some sense Afro-Caribbean or Pakistani-Muslim. It is not a new problem.

Summary and conclusion

What contribution do faith groups make towards social and community cohesion? We can summarize by saying that faith groups help to build both bonding and bridging social capital and therefore assist community cohesion. Religion, we can safely say, produces people who are 'unusually active social capitalists'.[52] However, there are trends affecting religion and spirituality that are eroding traditional forms of Christianity, and it is not easy to see what the outcome of these will be as organized religion both shrinks and adapts. It is possible that Christianity may cease to be a significant presence in many parts of the country within a relatively short period of time. It is equally possible that declining congregations may be replaced by more vibrant ones. However, the flourishing churches may turn out to be less community-minded and outward-looking, concentrating on evangelism and teaching rather than community engagement. Whether the minority faiths will be squeezed by the same secularizing tendencies is an open question. But for the moment, what we can say is that while faith may no longer be society's glue, it may yet be a sacred marinade in many communities. That is especially true of those religions that have come more recently to the UK and are associated with particular minority ethnic groups.

But what happens to communities if faith groups continue to remain in their own enclaves? How does that affect cohesion? This is a key question in many urban areas and is the subject of the next chapter.

3

Do 'parallel lives' threaten community cohesion?

———————

To be rooted is perhaps the most important and least recognized need of the human soul. *Simone Weil,* The Need for Roots

Two nations; between whom there is no intercourse and no sympathy; who are as ignorant of each other's habits, thoughts and feelings, as if they were dwellers in different zones, or inhabitants of different planets, who are formed by a different breeding, are fed a different food, are ordered by different manners, and are not governed by the same laws. *Benjamin Disraeli,* Sybil, or the Two Nations

Surveys of British born BME (black and minority ethnic) communities living in the UK show that people identify more with their local area and the place of origin of their family than Britain; surveys of white working-class people show that many no longer identify with their local area.

Alessandra Buonfino (with Louisa Thomson), for the
Commission on Integration and Cohesion

Those who reported on the summer disturbances of 2001 drew attention to two factors that they believed differentiated them from the riots of the 1980s: the spatial separation of the ethnic communities from one another and a religious or religious-cultural dimension. The different ethnic populations of the northern towns – white and Asian – lived 'parallel lives' that 'often do not seem to touch at any point, let alone overlap and promote any meaningful interchanges' – so said the independent review team set up by the government to draw lessons from what had taken place.[1] People were separated by race; they were also separated by religion – Christian and Muslim.[2] That there might be a religious dimension to Britain's social tensions was further highlighted by the terrorist outrage of 7 July 2005, which was certainly religiously motivated.

Since then, a perception has been growing among the non-Muslim population that the problems of extremism are principally located in (at least part of) the Muslim community, and that both the riots and the terrorism are symptomatic of a much wider and deeper problem posed, by some versions of Islamic faith, to social and community cohesion in liberal democracies – though not only liberal democracies, since Muslim states are equally at risk of attack. As a result, the government became more interested in the role that faith played in people's lives and whether interfaith activities and dialogue could significantly help in reducing the terrorist threat and in promoting greater cohesion.

It was against this background that I was asked, together with colleagues at Lancaster University, to undertake research into attitudes towards religion among young people in the different ethnic communities in the North West of England, and the extent and effectiveness of interfaith work.[3] We did this over two years, between 2006 and 2007, in Burnley and other northern towns; the research is known as the Burnley Project. In this chapter I want to draw on this research to address the question of whether these parallel existences matter for community cohesion. Is the cohesiveness of the community really undermined if white and Asian, Christian and Muslim, keep themselves to themselves? Does this separation impact on the two communities in the same way? I will set out what the research tells us and then, in the light of that, return to the wider discussion about what makes for cohesiveness.

Enclaved existence and parallel lives

Professor Ted Cantle's report into the disturbances in Oldham in 2001 used the term 'parallel lives' to draw attention to the fact that the Asian community there did not seem to be following the pattern of other post-war migrations. For example, in the inner-city area in Leicester in which I grew up, there had been a succession of mainly European immigrants – principally Poles and Ukrainians – who had come and settled in close proximity to one another just before and after the Second World War. This very soon affected everyday life for all of us, for example what was on sale in local food shops: we observed, and sometimes felt brave enough to try, unfamiliar types of sausage and jars of pickled cabbage. And there were particular

clubs and churches to which the immigrants gravitated and sometimes made their own. As a child I recall going a number of times
with friends of my family to the local Dom Kombatanta – a Polish
ex-servicemen's club – for a very lively social evening of Polish sing-
ing and dancing, eating and drinking. One Roman Catholic Church
offered services in Polish, and at least one Polish priest was always
resident in the presbytery. A number of those on the register of my
local primary school had Polish surnames. As a result of Poland
joining the European Union in 2004 there has been a more recent
influx of Polish workers, giving a new lease of life to the Polish
church, though whether these latest migrants will stay is an open
question. But the club closed many years ago and the older community itself has largely been assimilated, often as a result of intermarriage.[4] But in northern towns and cities the Pakistani Muslim
community has not dispersed and integrated into the wider society
but has remained separated and insular.[5] This seems to be less true
of other religious minorities – Hindus, Sikhs, Jains. Estate agents in
Leicester report that as these minority groups become more prosperous and aspirational they move out into other areas of the city or
beyond, and these areas are becoming ethnically more mixed.[6]
In this way they seem to be closer to the pattern of dispersal of
previous migrant groups. This does not seem to be the pattern for
the Pakistani Asians of Burnley.

The phenomenon of parallel lives began with spatial separation, white and Asian families living in separate parts of the town,
which I have called 'enclavization'. This residential enclavization,
then, has consequences for education, employment and integration. Enclavization is not segregation, if that implies an element
of compulsion or planning. Modern Britain does not deliberately
pursue policies of segregation. Rather, enclavization comes about
from a combination of economic and social factors and some personal choice – though these are different for the white and Asian
communities.

As far as the Asian community is concerned, enclavization follows from the availability of cheap housing – to rent or to buy – in
certain inner areas of the town and a desire to live near to family
and friends in the Pakistani community. As the community grows,
mosques, Islamic community centres and shops follow. Personal
choice in location is, in any case, restricted by relative poverty and

an inability to afford houses in more prosperous parts of town. The
spatial segregation is then compounded by 'white flight': with few
exceptions, the only white people remaining in the now predominantly Asian inner-area wards are the more elderly, who can as a
result feel trapped and isolated.[7]

In this respect, enclavization is the way in which migrating
groups have always behaved, at least initially. The history of the USA
in the late-nineteenth and early-twentieth century was exactly this,
as different ethnic groups moved to America in considerable numbers and made different parts of the cities their own. Between 1870
and 1900 – a mere 30 years – nearly 12 million people immigrated,
more than in the previous 250 years – Catholics and Jews, Europeans and Asians.[8] It led to a debate about what it was to be
American and whether it was necessary to speak English – a debate
that resembles the discussion we have been having for a year or
two now about multiculturalism and what it is to be British.

But in the case of the white enclaves, most people are there not
through choice but the lack of choice. The poorest families among
the white working class and non-working class have no choice other
than to live in those areas of the town where there is relatively cheap
private rented accommodation or social and council housing. One
consequence of the housing policies of the past few decades has
been to remove control of social housing from the local authority
and put it into the hands of housing associations and tenants themselves (through the right to buy). The downside of this is that a
crucial instrument of urban planning is lost to local authorities,
one unintended consequence of which is that racially mixed areas
are harder for them to achieve.[9] The white families in these enclaves
are those left behind in the economic race. Those who are in work
are often among the most badly paid, existing close to the minimum
wage; those who are unemployed seem to be almost unemployable,
with few educational qualifications or attainments – some are now
the second or third generation of unemployed. Many children in these
areas grow up with few aspirations and little belief in the ability
of the education system to change their lives for the better. When
I first visited Burnley for the purposes of the research, I was struck
both by how much this was like the white working-class area in
which I had grown up and also how unlike it it was in terms of
people's attitude towards the future. Unlike my parents' generation,

few here had any faith that hard work, politics or education offered them a way out of poverty or could make any significant difference to their lives or that of their neighbours.

Once enclaves are established they lead to parallel lives. As a result of spatial segregation, children go to more monocultural, mono-ethnic and monofaith schools. They grow up with friends of their own race, religion and culture. They begin to socialize with people who are exclusively like themselves. Whenever they can, they seek employment in places where their cultural group is predominant. This raises the important question of the values and attitudes that such enclaved existence creates and perpetuates. Does it make community cohesion more difficult?

The Burnley Project

The Lancaster research was designed to discover whether interfaith activity made a difference to the attitudes that the different ethnic and religious groups had towards one another in these enclaved areas. Two different methodological approaches were used.[10] First, data was collected by a social-science researcher, Dr Andrew Holden, from 40 young people in the Burnley area, aged 18–30, by means of semi-structured, taped interviews of one hour. This gave qualitative data on their attitudes towards faith and their involvement with faith groups and interfaith activities. Second, a questionnaire was given to several hundred schoolchildren in Burnley and Blackburn designed to discover how far they embraced attitudes and values that were essential for social and community cohesion – liberal, tolerant, integrative, humanistic. It was important to target young people, white and Asian, both because it was mainly young people from both communities that rioted in 2001, and because they are the next generation of adults and leaders in the community. We wanted to examine the extent to which the perception the two groups had of each other was influenced by their faith. The 40 interviewees were selected from a number of different places of worship and secular organizations linked to the voluntary sector. They were young men and women, white and Asian in equal numbers, Muslim and Christian, though we also included young people who had no faith since it was important to test how far faith was or was not a factor in creating values that strengthened cohesion.

We noted one immediate difference between the two groups: the Asian young people were more inclined to express their identity in terms of faith. They all described themselves as 'Muslim' as well as 'Asian', though there were varying degrees of religious conviction and practice – some would not necessarily see religious adherence as the most important aspect of their identity. Both white and Asian varied in their attitude towards interfaith dialogue and activity – some could see a point to it and some could not. This suggests first that we should be wary of defining people solely by self-ascribed religious affiliation; identities in modern societies are far more complex. It also suggests that if greater cohesion is to be achieved in towns with pronounced enclavization, faith is not the only cause of division. There are also matters of class, gender, ethnicity and neighbourhood.

The 40 participants were interviewed individually and asked a series of questions about their lives as Burnley residents. At the beginning of the interviews, they were asked to share their biographical narratives; that is, details of family relationships, childhood memories, educational experiences and personal and professional development since leaving school. The interviews then progressed to questions of a more existential nature: participants described their faith perspectives and gave an account of their faith journey. They were all asked about their perceptions of interfaith activities and what they felt faith communities could contribute to social cohesion. Those with faith convictions were asked to comment on other faiths and to identify any similarities that they felt existed between Burnley's two main faith groups. The most important questions concerned the amount of contact, voluntary or otherwise, that the interviewees had with members of other faith and ethnic communities.

The degree of engagement with religious institutions – whether church or mosque – varied considerably among those who said they were religious. But even those who had no faith could appreciate the value of faith and the role it played in the lives of others where they had contact with people of faith. It is probably true to say that neither policy-makers nor faith groups working in interfaith contexts have made much of an attempt to understand how faith perspectives come to be acquired or how they impact on social relations. In Burnley, young adults' perceptions of faith and its potential to create a better society varied in accordance with locality and with the nature of interaction between faith and secular communities. But we drew the following broad conclusions:

- In the case of the white majority, even those with no religious faith were able to recognize the importance of faith in the lives of others as long as they had an appreciation of cultural diversity and had frequent contact with members of other ethnic/religious groups. (The existence of the enclave, therefore, poses a problem.)
- In most Muslim communities there is a delicate interplay between religious, cultural and national identity (influenced to a greater or lesser extent by relations with the non-Muslim population) that highlights the need for religious and ethnic communities to engage more positively with each other. (Again, the enclave stands in the way of contact.)
- People of no faith need to be more aware of those aspects of the various faiths that can be used to promote integrative and cohesive values and beat down prejudice.

In addition to the interviews with young adults, we also administered a questionnaire among Year 10 students in three types of community school – schools where the admission authority is the local council not the school or some religious foundation – one in Burnley and two in the comparator town of Blackburn.[11] The three types of school were: (a) predominantly ethnically white; (b) predominantly ethnically Asian; (c) ethnically mixed Asian and white.

In contrast to the interviews with young adults, the questionnaire collected data from a much larger group (some 435 pupils) in their penultimate year of compulsory education in North-West towns. The majority of these students were aged 15 at the time of the survey. One of the key aims of the survey was to establish the relationship between tolerance shown towards other faiths and social group membership; hence, the schools chosen each recruited pupils from very different faith and ethnic backgrounds.

A significant minority of young people from school type (a) (white) showed attitudes that were not at all conducive to community cohesion. They were intolerant of people of other races, faiths and cultures; they saw little reason to study or respect other (non-Christian) faiths; they thought their own ethnic group was superior to others; and so on. We see here fertile soil for the views of the extreme right in British politics.

Pupils of school type (b) (Asian) were the opposite. On the whole they were tolerant of people of other races, faiths and cultures; they saw every reason to study and respect other faiths; they did not think their own ethnic group was superior to others; and so on. Those in school type (c) (mixed) produced a more mixed picture, though on the whole they were nearer to school type (b) than (a).

Research conclusions

The research findings suggest a number of things that have both a direct and an indirect bearing on the matter of social and community cohesion, some helpful and some not. I will first discuss what I think it tells us about the Pakistani Asian community, then the white community, and then what I believe are the consequences for both if enclavization continues.

In the first place, we may assume that the young people who were surveyed broadly reflected the views of their parents and respective communities. If this is the case, the majority of Asian families in the northern towns we have researched probably feel 'at home' in Britain. This ought not to surprise: these families chose to come to the UK not only for economic reasons but because this was a freer atmosphere in which to live than a society more subject to conservative religious pressures. This is not to say that they are not relatively conservative in religious matters, but they prefer to choose to be conservative than have it thrust upon them. This is in line with other research that has found that the overwhelming majority of Muslims regard themselves as British and have no desire to be socially isolated.[12] This means that they will continue to feel settled and secure as long as they are treated fairly and well and not discriminated against.

For young Muslim Asians, growing up in an Asian enclave has provided them with a place of relative safety, a congenial environment for their early formative years in which they have been schooled in broadly integrative values by their families, the mosque and the school. As far as the inculcation of cohesive attitudes and values is concerned, enclavization is not a problem. There is also other qualitative research that suggests that enclavization in most British cities does not adversely affect how Asian families feel towards British society.[13] They can live separate lives yet still feel that they belong.

Enclavization also enables the Muslim community to retain its young people more successfully than perhaps it could if the Muslim population were more dispersed. There will be a certain peer pressure to go along to the mosque or the Qur'anic school. Families are aware of any backsliding on the part of neighbours and can encourage or cajole them into fulfilling their religious responsibilities. Imams or chairs of mosque committees can call on members and maintain their interest and enthusiasm. In these respects, the enclaved Muslim communities of Britain's towns and cities have all the characteristics, for good or ill, of the village. One helpful consequence of this – clearly revealed in the research – is that Asian young people who grew up in a religious household, attended the mosque and had good religious teaching at school had very positive attitudes towards not just their own faith but all faiths. Religion was valued and there was a curiosity to know more about people of other faiths. (The Chief Rabbi, Jonathan Sacks, writing about his childhood, witnesses to this. His parents sent their children to the local school, a Christian foundation (rather than a Jewish school), where he encountered teachers 'who valued their religion', as a result of which 'we learnt to value our own' and that of others as well.[14]

However, in the second place, the research findings would indicate a continuing threat to cohesion from the enclavization of the ethnically white communities in towns such as Burnley, Oldham and Bradford. Most of the young people – and we assume the community from which they came – had little contact with any Christian church, let alone any other faith, and the attitudes and values expressed by a significant minority were in many respects not conducive to social or community cohesion in a multifaith, multicultural society. Moreover, it would seem that the views they had absorbed in the home were too firmly entrenched to be overturned by any work the school might do. They are growing up with all the discontents that were on display at the time of the riots.

In other words, while enclavization may not be an issue for community cohesion as far as Asian young people are concerned, it is an issue for some white young people – and that ultimately has consequences for both communities when young people enter the more adult world, and do begin to cross each other's paths. At this point, young Muslim Asians begin to experience white racism for themselves. As long as enclavization continues, the different communities will continue to live parallel lives, with all the risk that entails – an unchallenged white racism and crises of identity for some young people, white and Asian, as they leave the protective environment of childhood. If there were to be disturbances again, it could hardly come as a surprise.

Enclavization has a further consequence. The liberal state exists to protect the individual from the exercise of undue power by both the state itself and also groups within the state, including cultural and religious communities. So, for example, a particular community may have traditional teachings about women or homosexuality that if acted upon would result in discrimination. The liberal state seeks to protect individuals from cultural or religious discrimination. But where cultural and religious groups live in enclaved communities, inevitably there is pressure from them to elevate the rights of the group – to teach and practise their traditions – over the rights of the individual not to be bound by them. We have already heard calls in some parts of Europe for Sharia to be operated on a local basis where Muslims are in a majority. This is where the doctrine of multiculturalism can create a problem if it is taken to mean that different cultures and their practices are to be so privileged that some individuals feel pressurized by their faith communities to conform. This would undermine the liberal values of the British state, and that would not be conducive to cohesion. There are liberal values that challenge some traditional teachings and practices in all religions, and those values must prevail.

Interfaith dialogue

This raises the question of whether the gap between the different ethnic and faith communities can be significantly bridged through interfaith dialogue – if by that we include any interfaith activity that leads to more and better mutual understanding between the different faith groups. The government certainly thinks so, and is developing its own interfaith strategy, though building on and not ignoring what is already in place – Gordon Brown has said that he would like to see an interfaith council in every community.[15] Interfaith groups are now active in many parts of the country, though by no means all. The earliest interfaith group was the Council of Christians and Jews, set up in 1942 to overcome the anti-Semitism that

had disfigured European life for much of the twentieth century
and culminated in the Holocaust.[16] The Inter Faith Network, which
seeks to promote contact between all faiths and offers all religious
communities support, has been in existence since 1987. As well as
having a national and regional structure, it also numbers over 200
local groups in its membership, drawing together people from all
the main faith communities – Baha'i, Buddhist, Christian, Hindu,
Jain, Jewish, Muslim, Sikh and Zoroastrian.[17] Many have been established since the events of 2001. The Network is unique in Europe.
Other interfaith groups – there are over 20 nationally – include the
Three Faiths Forum, founded in 1997 to bring together those monotheistic faiths that trace their descent from the patriarch Abraham
(Judaism, Christianity and Islam) and, more recently, the Christian
Muslim Forum (2005). There is no doubt that interfaith activities
of various kinds can play a part in establishing contacts between at
least some members of the different faith communities. During the
course of our research we came across many initiatives, including a
very active local interfaith group, Building Bridges Burnley (BBB).
This was set up after the riots, and brought together on a regular basis
the lay and clerical leaderships of mosques and churches. We could
summarize the contribution that interfaith activity makes in this
way:

- It brings together leaders of the faith communities and builds
  personal friendships and trust between them at different levels –
  national, regional, local.[18]
- This mutual recognition and respect enables the more recent and
  less established communities (those associated with the post-war
  migrations) to feel affirmed and valued without being patronized,
  and gradually to build their own capacity.
- It enables the newer communities to be part of the extensive networking that local religious leaders build up.
- When working well, interfaith groups create opportunities for
  different faith communities to get to know and understand one
  another better through shared social and cultural (and sometimes
  religious) events.
- It can provide channels of communication between less established or less confident faith communities and other agencies –
  such as the police, the local authority, the media.

- In times of community tension these friendships and channels of communication can play a valuable role, though they have to be fostered well before times of difficulty arise.
- At the national level, interfaith organizations can provide invaluable advice to government and other national bodies.

The above makes it clear why the government sees interfaith activities as having a role to play in building community cohesion and resilience, and why in 2007 it invested £13.8 million in the Faith Communities Capacity Building Fund, designed to enhance the ability of faith organizations to play a greater part in civil society, not least in conjunction with other faith groups.

Different interfaith groups are at different levels of engagement. It takes a long time to develop the degree of trust necessary for real exchange between people. Even then it is not easy to broach with one another the issues that divide and the issues that disturb. We have found that interfaith activities largely appeal to first- rather than second-generation migrants; but it is the second generation that is most susceptible to radicalization.

We should not exaggerate what interfaith involvement can do. In particular we need to recognize that the numbers involved in organized religion may be relatively modest. The number of observant Christians as a proportion of the population as a whole, as we saw in a previous chapter, may now be in the region of 6–12 per cent. This in itself is not a large proportion, while the white working and white non-working class will be significantly under-represented within even that – in very low single figures in many areas. The best guess for the number of regular attenders at the mosque may be about 30 per cent, though this has to be treated with a measure of caution since mosques do not keep records of attendance in the way that some churches record communicant or other figures. All the mosques that we contacted reported a falling away of young boys after the age of about 15. The numbers involved in interfaith activity, therefore, will be even smaller. Some Christians – principally evangelical and Pentecostal churches – and some Muslims – those mosques in the Deoband tradition – may be unwilling on doctrinal grounds to participate at all in interfaith dialogue or activity. Each would regard the other as dangerously idolatrous.

However, our general opinion arising from the Burnley Project is that the most effective form of interfaith work is what happens in schools. This is the one time in everyone's life when issues of faith can be raised in a fairly protective environment. An attempt can be made to help young people of different faiths, and none, understand the importance of faith in many people's lives and to give them some knowledge and appreciation of faiths other than their own. This is done formally in the religious education period. But in areas where there is more than one faith community, the informal contact between people of different religions, supported by classroom teaching, is invaluable. The separation of children by race and religion as a result of enclavization represents, therefore, a missed opportunity for strengthening community cohesion at an early stage.

The roots/routes of extremism

The Burnley Project findings may also be giving us some pointers towards some of the mechanisms whereby some white young people become extremist, attracted to the politics of the extreme right, and why some Muslim young people embrace terrorism – and perhaps a link between the two.

The most worrying result came from the type (a) schools, where white young people have few or no relationships with those of other ethnicities, cultures or faiths (though as a matter of fact few seemed to have any contact with organized Christianity). What this means is that prejudices are never put to the test; friendships across the boundaries of race, faith and culture are never made; the values and attitudes of parents are internalized and never challenged, other than theoretically by the school.

We tend to assume that the only young people who have a serious crisis of identity are those from the ethnic minorities. This is not true. White young people from enclaved areas are also asking questions about what it means to be British – but to be British and white. Yet they receive little or no help as they struggle, principally because identity is not seen as an issue for them or because their attempts to articulate their concerns – about immigration, jobs, the nature of society – are misconstrued as provocations. However, when these young white boys and girls, from relatively poor backgrounds, try to make sense of their experience, there is one group of people who will have answers for them: representatives of the extreme right. The young people may well find in their ideology a seductive, congenial and coherent account of their experiences and the nature of the society around them. It goes like this: 'Look around. Despite the fact that your (white and Christian) forebears made Britain prosperous and powerful, you are not sharing that prosperity. Job prospects for you are poor. You are compelled to live underprivileged lives. Why? Because people of another ethnicity and religion (Asian and Muslim), only recently settled in the country, are allowed to take jobs and houses and to do at least as well and sometimes better than you. Moreover, the public bodies will bend over backwards to help them, though not you – which is why education and working hard brings few rewards to people like you. In addition, the liberal establishment will conspire together to try to prevent these issues being discussed.' This account makes sense of their lives – it is coherent; and in a strange way enables them to retain some dignity – it is congenial. It is seductive because it suggests that their misfortune is not their fault (which would be an alternative account) but someone else's – immigrants or those from immigrant-descended families and the 'establishment'. It feeds resentment, and no amount of teaching on citizenship or the values of neighbourliness will overcome these perceptions from the enclave. The first result of enclavization is not so much white racism – though it does produce that – as a culture of resignation and resentment with all its smouldering discontents. The enclave does little or nothing to raise the sights of these young people, or to suggest that through education or hard work their lives could be made significantly different from those of their parents. As long as the enclave remains, the risk will be that this culture of sullen discontent will prove incapable of being significantly changed.

This is surely one of the biggest cultural changes that has overtaken the British people in my lifetime – the emergence of a section of the white working class that seems to have turned its back on the traditional routes out of poverty – education and employment.

The results from type (b) schools, however, pose a more difficult question about Muslim extremism. How and why do some young people (principally men) lose these liberal, humanistic and integrative values that they clearly have at school and become radicalized?

Our best guess from the research – and it is only a guess until it can be tested – is that pupils in predominantly Asian schools absorb the values and attitudes of their parents, which are broadly liberal – very positive about Britain, not dismissive of other faiths and cultures, though wary of some aspects of British society. (Their parents, who have come to Britain from Pakistan, tend to be the more entrepreneurial and attracted by Western society; in some instances, as I have said, they come to get away from a more tightly controlled theocratic society, though without completely breaking their links.) These liberal values are reinforced in the mosque and the school and not seriously challenged or tested until the young people leave school. However, when as older teenagers or young adults they leave the comparatively safe environments of home, mosque and school for work, college and the social life of the town centre, they begin to encounter for the first time, and at first hand, white prejudice and racism and a morality or immorality that can be distressing. This leads them to reflect more widely on the position of Muslims in contemporary Britain – and around the world.

Unlike their parents, who may have come to the UK with lower expectations, these Asian young people have grown up here and have the same expectations and aspirations as their white peers. The first experiences of racism are shocking and disappointing. It is encountered in many ways and contexts: taunts and comments; physical attack; the perception that jobs or promotion are influenced by ethnicity; the belief that while protection is given under the law to Christians (blasphemy laws – though this is no longer the case) and Jews and Sikhs (race relations), no such protection exists for Muslims; the perception that Muslims are badly treated across the world (the Gulf Wars and military action in Afghanistan fall into this category); stop-and-search by the police; suspicion and hostility; and so on. Most of the actual or perceived discrimination is fairly 'low level'. Even so, it can create a profound crisis of identity: 'If I can be treated this way in my own town and country, is it really possible to be British and Muslim?' The underlying anxiety is that it calls into question the understanding of the UK as a community of fairness and equal opportunities – which is what the home, the school and the mosque have taught. The danger lies in the fact that at this point in their lives these young people may not have anyone on hand to help them think through the issues and their experiences – they are not in school, they may not be comfortable turning to family, they may have little contact with mosque leaders, who may in any case not appreciate the problem or have the skills to deal with it and, if they are within the criminal justice system, there may be little understanding of what may be happening to them and quite possibly no check on who is saying what to them.

Part of this struggle to understand what it is to be British and Muslim may also lead them to reflect on what is widely seen in many parts of the Muslim community as British moral laxity. They observe youths drinking heavily or indulging in drugs in town centres or suburban shopping malls after dark, or scantily dressed young women heading towards the bright lights on Friday and Saturday evenings.

Asian young people respond to this crisis of identity and the tension it creates in different ways. Some continue to hold to liberal values, recognizing white racism as disfiguring British society but not endemic or fundamental to it, and live with the tension of belonging to a minority that can sometimes be discriminated against. Some seek to dissolve the tension by assimilating into the wider community, abandoning their Islamic traditions. Others find a new sense of identity, meaning and self-worth by asserting their faith and culture, adopting a more conservative expression of Islam, sometimes more conservative than their parents. For some women this may mean taking up forms of Islamic dress, such as the *hijab* or *niqab*. For both men and women it means worrying much more about what in modern British life is *haram* (forbidden) and what is *halal* (allowed) according to Muslim law – as questions to Muslim internet sites show. In other words, there can be radicalization without extremism. On the contrary, these pious young Muslims are determined to follow the *sunna* of the Prophet by being model husbands and wives, neighbours and citizens: the behaviour of the terrorists and the theological shallowness of their justifications appals them. While they may describe themselves as Muslim first and British second, they are nevertheless committed to the UK, though they regret that many of its standards – such as the immodesty of women – fall way below what the Qur'an expects. But they can live with the tension implicit in the question, 'Can I be Muslim and British?' because they realize that multiple identity is possible; and multiple identity, which we all have in a plural society, creates tensions.

A few take a different route as a result of meeting travelling teachers (not the local imams) or joining certain societies or viewing certain sites on the internet. From them they will have another theology/ideology available that has real allure: an extreme form of theo-political Islam that makes sense of the experiences of young Muslims in a quite different way. Racism and disappointment are explained as the failure of British society to live by the Qur'an. The worldwide Muslim community is idealized as the universal *umma*, but greater emphasis is placed on the coming time when the UK (and the whole world) will be part of a Muslim caliphate – a theocracy. Moreover, in the struggle – *jihad* – to bring this about, violence is permissible. All of this has the potential to give the young Muslim a sense of real worth and importance as an agent of the future Islamic realm. It also dissolves the tension implicit in the question, 'Can I be Muslim and British?' by suggesting that one cannot be both; multiple identity is impossible; a choice has to be made. From the moment that this extreme strain of Islam is embraced, the adherent ceases to have loyalties to the UK and to fellow Britons, even to members of his own family or local community. His loyalties are only to the idealized fiction of the *umma*. We can say, therefore, that a second danger of enclavization is that a few young Muslims will be not only radicalized but also drawn into extremism if the only theology available to them to explain their experiences – especially their negative experiences – is that of the extremist groups.

The Burnley Project findings suggest that after a certain age – somewhere in the middle teenage years – many young Muslims begin to have little contact with their local mosques. We also note that the young people's knowledge of Islam is not very profound. (Most of the after-school religious education seems to consist of the rote learning of the Arabic Qur'an.) This means that as they begin to wrestle with the question of identity – 'What is it to be Muslim and British?' – they have few theological resources to help them. In any case, unlike Judaism, which has had longer to work out how to be Jewish and British, there is little home-grown Islamic theology to resource them and few teachers with the skills to do the necessary work. The paucity of written material for them to draw upon stands in some contrast to the sheer number of books and pamphlets available expounding some of the more extreme forms of Islam – the *Salafi* and *Wahabbi* traditions – funded largely by Saudi Arabia.

This is also an argument for ensuring, wherever possible, that early schooling is in mixed schools – white and Asian. Asian young people in mixed schools encounter racism earlier in life and have to learn to deal with it in the playground. When this happens, parents and schoolteachers are on hand to be supportive and to reinforce the commitment nevertheless to integrative values. The earlier young people are exposed to the kind of low-level ethnic prejudice that may always be a feature of any racially mixed society, the better. They not only need liberal values; they also need to develop early skills in dealing with racism and prejudice without losing faith in liberal society. (This is not to say that early exposure infallibly inoculates Muslim young people against extremist views, since there are many routes to extremism. Mohammad Sidique Khan, for example, the mastermind behind the 7 July 2005 London bombings, was educated at a predominantly white primary school.[19])

All of this suggests that if an overriding policy goal of the school system is to contribute towards community cohesion, every effort should be made to prevent monocultural/monoethnic schools from developing. This creates a dilemma with regard to faith schools since they may become monocultural/monoethnic as a result of being monofaith. As with many policy options, different though equally desirable objectives may not be mutually reinforcing. Faith schools are wanted by parents. There is some evidence that they drive up standards. Moreover, the above results of the Year 10 questionnaires in predominantly Asian (Muslim) schools – that is, schools whose profile was almost that of a faith school – would lead us to suppose that faith schools are more likely to produce young people who espouse integrative values since faith schools take seriously and value not only their own faith but the faith of others. It was the type (a) schools – where few had any serious contact with organized religion of any kind – that produced young people who were dismissive of other cultures and faiths. If faith schools are to be opposed it cannot be because empirically they produce young people less willing to integrate, because probably they do not, but on the quite different grounds that they do nothing to prepare Asian young people for racism later in life.

In a recent report from the think tank Policy Exchange, much was made of the finding that a majority of Muslim young people wanted to live under Sharia law.[20] We would suggest that this may not be all that it seems. (It is, in any case, hard to know what was being asked since Sharia is not a simple and universal set of pre-scriptions and injunctions.) What young Muslims may mean by this is that they want to live in a society that observes God's laws and mirrors the practice (*sunna*) of the Prophet. This is the correct answer of piety. In this respect they may be little different from young Christians who might say they too wanted to live 'under God's laws'. But it needs testing. Young people need to be asked more specific questions about the actual content of Sharia or other Muslim practices – government by clergy, submitting to clerical *fatwas*, multiple wives for men, discrimination against women in family courts and so on, before we can be sure that this is what they want. When the specifics are made clear the enthusiasm may be tempered and the 'Yes' to Sharia significantly qualified.

The Burnley Project research among young people suggests to us that the overwhelming majority of Muslims are happy with humanistic and integrative values and the institutions of the democratic state. But while they may as individuals want to live by liberal values, the religious and cultural communities from which they come are not always or in all respects liberal. At this point, the British government and other public bodies need to be very clear that their commitment is to uphold those values in the face of pressures from more traditional community groups that do not share them.

There was, however, one final result of the research that was in-triguing. This was that in answer to a question about where author-ity lay for young people in ethical matters, both the (Muslim) Asian and the (Christian) white young people indicated that they wanted to make up their own minds. In this respect the Asian youngsters were becoming more like their (more secular) white counterparts. In both communities there seems to be a move away from accepting without question the teachings of religious (or any other) authority, though this is more pronounced in the white community. It is poss-ible that this may be one of the most important findings. It would seem to bear out the fears expressed by a number of Muslim leaders that many older teenagers are less visible in the mosques and less willing to receive advice from them. This points to the next genera-tion of Asian adults being very different from the generation before them.

Summary and conclusion

We began this chapter with a question: 'Do parallel lives threaten community cohesion?' Research has shown that where people have friends from other ethnic backgrounds, they are more likely to develop attitudes and values that promote a more cohesive society.[21] On the face of it, therefore, enclavization would seem to work against cohesion. The Burnley Project research, however, presents policy-makers with something of a dilemma. This arises from the different effects of enclavization on the white and Asian populations as we observed it among young people. On the one hand, the enclave provides a safe environment for the Asian Muslim population. This was very important in an earlier period, when many families were newly arrived in Britain. By living in close proximity to one another, bonding social capital (see Chapter 2) was built, and that was of crucial importance in helping to turn immigrant labourers into settled ethnic minorities. The enclave has enabled the Asian community to feel rooted and at home; and feeling rooted, as Simone Weil reminded us at the head of this chapter, is the first 'need of the soul'. It also contributes towards bridging social capital (again, see Chapter 2) by giving the growing generation of young people positive attitudes towards those of other faiths and ethnicities. If the Asian Muslims had been more diffused among the population, these positive results might have been more difficult to achieve.

On the other hand, however, the enclave has stoked white resentment among some of those who have not greatly prospered in contemporary Britain, and this has done nothing to reduce ethnic tensions. Poorer white families have watched with growing resentment considerable sums of public money being spent in the Asian parts of the town – spent, of course, not because they were Asian but because the aim was to target and regenerate the most deprived areas – and have interpreted this as 'favouring' Asians/Muslims, a type of reverse racism. Government at every level has not always been sensitive to how schemes and initiatives are perceived among the various social groups that make up the urban areas. Enclavization does nothing to break down these discontents, which erode any sense of community solidarity.[22]

In addition, enclavization may also have made the experiences of Asian young people more difficult when they have to leave the more protective environment of home–mosque–school to go to college or begin work. Encounters with white racist attitudes at this point leave them open to influence by people with other agendas, mirror-images of the right-wing propagandists who are always waiting to influence the minds of disappointed and resentful young white people.

The answer to the question, 'Do parallel lives threaten community cohesion?' is a disappointing 'Yes' and 'No'. But if the question is altered a little to become, 'What could ameliorate the worst effects of enclavization?' the answer would be: patiently continue with policies designed to overcome racism but also increase the number of mixed schools or, if this is not possible without drawing up unrealistic catchment area boundaries, increase the possibilities for young people of different faiths and cultures to meet and mingle with each other early – in playgrounds, classrooms and sports fields – on a systematic and regular basis, through school linking.[23] For the most important way of increasing mutual understanding will be done face-to-face, before young people leave school.

But is this being too optimistic? Does not religion by virtue of its exclusivity, or at least some versions of some religions, contribute towards undermining any attempt to build cohesive communities? This is the hard question we turn to next.

4

Does religion threaten community cohesion?

----◆◆◆----

I pledge allegiance to the flag of the United States of America and to the Republic for which it stands, one nation under God, indivisible, with liberty and justice for all.

American school students' daily pledge

Our so-called scholars today are content with their Toyotas and semi-detached houses. They seem to think that their responsibilities lie in pleasing the *kufr* [unbelievers] instead of Allah. So they tell us ludicrous things, like you must obey the law of the land. Praise be God! How did we ever conquer lands in the past if we were to obey this law?   *From Mohammad Sidique Khan's suicide video speech*

Tantum religio potuit suadere malorum.[1]   *Lucretius*

During the course of my lifetime – roughly the period since the end of the Second World War – the social landscape of Britain has been transformed out of all recognition. The country in which I spent my earliest years was essentially monoethnic, monocultural and monophonic; it was white, Protestant and English-speaking. The country I live in today is multiethnic and multicultural, and while English is the principal language of communication, many languages are in fact spoken and catered for – every public institution from the law courts to the National Health Service makes some provision for languages other than English – though whether this aids community cohesion is itself currently an issue (some would argue that if people are to integrate successfully they must be encouraged to learn English). In London it is estimated that there are more than 40 communities of foreign origin, made up of at least ten thousand members, while in the capital's schools over 300 different languages are spoken in the playground. Even some of the older native

73

languages of these islands are reviving. We recognize that we now live in a world where large numbers of people are always going to be on the move, migrating from country to country and continent to continent as never before. In 2005, for example, an estimated 565,000 people entered the country and 380,000 left. As far as religion is concerned, those of us who live in urban areas are not at all surprised when another new mosque, temple or gurdwara appears somewhere in the city.

For more than half a century the people of the UK have been attempting to build capacity and learn how to live as a multiethnic, multicultural and multifaith nation, preparing ourselves for the new world of the twenty-first century. The question of community cohesion arises out of this changed situation. What many are not sure about is whether religion helps or hinders the attempt to make the new Britain cohesive; or rather, a growing number of people seem to believe that religion seriously undermines cohesion – and they have plenty of examples to submit in evidence. In this chapter I will consider some specific instances that have caused alarm, before turning in the final chapter to consider the more general argument that every religion that makes exclusive claims to ultimate truth is by its very nature destabilizing in a plural society.

Common perceptions of religion

The question, 'Does religion undermine cohesion?' is asked by people who would regard themselves as in some sense 'religious', as well as by those who have no time for religious faith. We have already considered in an earlier chapter the positive contribution that religion can make; but is there another side to the story, and does the negative outweigh the positive? There seems to be a prima facie case to answer.[2] After all, has not religion blighted community life in Northern Ireland for much of the post-war period? Did it not create havoc in Bosnia? Is it not a critical factor in the never-ending cycle of mayhem and violence in Gaza and the West Bank? Lucretius certainly thought religion was a problem.

This is also the starting-point for much contemporary secular, anti-religious writing and sentiment. Religion is portrayed as some terrible virus infecting people and making them aggressive and hostile towards those who do not share their certainties and perspective on the world. This is the view of Richard Dawkins and Christopher Hitchens.[3] Dawkins said this in a conversation with Sue Lawley when he appeared on BBC Radio 4's *Desert Island Discs* programme in 1995:

> Certainly (religion) can be positively harmful in various ways, obviously in causing wars, which has happened often enough in history, causing fatwas, causing people to do ill to one another because they are so convinced that they know what is right. Because they feel it from inside – they've been told from within themselves what is right – anything goes – you can kill people because you know that they're wrong. That is certainly evil.

The views expressed here probably now form part of a generally accepted assumption among contemporary intellectuals about the nature of religion: it has been a force for evil in the world. It is a view often stated as if it were self-evidently true and did not invite contradiction – hence Dawkins' saying the harmfulness of religion was 'obvious'.[4] In this chapter, however, I want to examine this assumption.

But the danger with asking the question, 'Does religion undermine cohesion?' is that we begin to answer it in a very generalized and theoretical way. But from a more sociological point of view, specific contexts are what matter. The question is not whether some hypothetical understanding of religion threatens some hypothetical community but whether in the particular circumstances of the UK in the early years of the twenty-first century, religion presents or might present any sort of threat to community cohesion. Or to put this question another way, despite the warnings of Richard Dawkins and others, 'Given that religion mainly does not seem to offer a threat to community cohesion in the UK, under what particular circumstances might it do so?'

Before examining that question, however, we might pause briefly to consider an alternative perspective to the one offered by those who see religion as an inevitable cause of social and community woes. This is the idea that it is not religion per se but human nature that is the problem; religion provides, as it were, an excuse. Those who argue in this way would see all human society as vulnerable to the struggles for power or influence of the groups it comprises. Every society, however homogeneous it may seem, is capable at any moment of tearing itself apart – we can see this happen whenever the forces of law and order break down. Those who argue in this way would have no difficulty in pointing to Iraq after the fall of Saddam Hussein as vindication. In the ensuing power vacuum, groups that had previously lived (relatively) peacefully side by side were suddenly at each other's throats. Similarly in Yugoslavia, when the central authority of the communist regime collapsed, the country divided along the most bitter tribal lines.

When a group of people distinguish between themselves and the other, one marker of difference – and a very potent marker – might be religion. So in Northern Ireland the contending groups badged themselves 'Catholic' and 'Protestant', even though the dispute between them was not really about religion but about access to political power and the distribution of wealth and opportunity that flowed from that. Of course, for some it was also about religion. The Revd Ian Paisley frequently spoke of the political struggle in religious terms, at least in the first part of his political career. The Loyalist cause was God's cause:

> God has a people in this province. There are more born-again people in Ulster to the square mile than anywhere else in the world. This little province had the peculiar preservation of divine Providence. You only have to read the history of Ulster to see time after time when it seemed humanly impossible to extract Ulster from seeming disaster, that God intervened. Why? God has a purpose for this province, and this plant of Protestantism sown here in the north-eastern part of this island. The enemy has tried to root it out, but still it grows today, and I believe, like a grain of mustard seed, its future is going to be mightier yet. God who made her mighty will make her mightier yet in his Divine will.[5]

This is a heady mix of politics and religion, with allusions to the Bible and patriotic songs – 'Land of Hope and Glory'. But few outside Paisley's own party (and probably not everyone within it) would see the issues in religious terms, and almost none in the Nationalist camp; neither Sinn Fein nor the Provisional IRA thought the struggle was anything other than political. Nevertheless, the Province is a more religious culture than the mainland, so that while this rhetoric would resonate for some in Northern Ireland it would cut little ice anywhere else in the UK.

In the Holy Land the issue is about different ethnic groups occupying the same small area – about the size of Wales – and competing for its scarce resources of land and water. The protagonists happen to be (mainly) Muslim Arabs and Jews, secular and religious, which enables religion to be used as a marker of difference and a means of motivation. But religion could not be used in this way in the dispute between Basque separatists and non-separatists in Spain since the Catholic faith was common to all.

Perhaps all we need to do as far as this argument goes is to note that even if the tension between people is not at root religious, religion can be enlisted in a cause and, when it is, it may make the settling of matters more complex and difficult. The question then is, 'Under what circumstances, if at all, could religion become an issue for cohesion in the UK, given that the country is now multi-faith?'

This is not a completely hypothetical question since we have already witnessed three types of situation where religion has revealed the potentiality for divisions between us, and social and community cohesion seems to have been strained. In ascending order of concern these are: a debate around the role of religion in determining public policy where there are ethical issues; the place of Sharia in non-Islamic states; and the issue of religious extremism. I will consider each in turn.

Organized religion and public policy

In 2007, following two years of consultation, the Human Fertilization and Embryology Bill was introduced into Parliament. The legislation was designed to do a number of things, including: ensuring that all human embryos outside the body were subject to regulation; allowing 'inter-species' embryos created from human and animal genetic material for research into illnesses such as Alzheimer's, Parkinson's and motor neurone disease; recognizing same-sex couples as the legal parents of children born by means of donated sperm, eggs and embryos. Some of the key provisions of the bill were opposed by the Roman Catholic Church, whose natural-law approach to ethics generally makes it resistant to anything that interferes with the 'natural' rhythms of life and death – contraception, abortion, euthanasia. In the case of this bill, it objected to those clauses that permitted the insertion of human DNA into an empty animal egg in order to produce stem cells for studying diseases and developing therapies. It is not my purpose to debate the merits of the bill and what it allowed and regulated but only to note the situation that this created for Roman Catholic MPs. This became very clear on Easter Day 2008, when at least three senior bishops of the Roman Catholic Church denounced the legislation and called upon Roman Catholic MPs to 'obey their Christian consciences' and defeat the bill, which would have precipitated the resignation of those who were members of the government. The language some of the hierarchy used was unusually strong. Cardinal Keith O'Brien, Archbishop of St Andrews and Edinburgh, said in an Easter sermon that what was proposed was a 'monstrous attack on human rights, human dignity and human life' that would allow 'experiments of Frankenstein proportion'. His comments dominated news reports across the Easter weekend. A head of steam developed. Unusually and controversially, a representative of the Sikh community, Indarjit Singh, used a slot on Radio 4's 'Thought for the Day' to object as well. His words were as shocking as Archbishop O'Brien's and he may have taken his cue from them:

> There is also the fear that over the years, in the interest of life enhancement, we have been inching away from a previously accepted view of the sanctity of human life. If, for example, the research now being contemplated had been conducted by Hitler's scientists in the 1940s, it would in all probability have been universally condemned.[6]

There seems little doubt that the Archbishop and Indarjit Singh had misunderstood the bill. Lord Winston, an expert on issues of human fertilization, said the Scottish prelate was 'lying' and 'misleading', and Sir Leszek Borysiewicz, chief executive of the Medical Research Council and a Roman Catholic, said that what was proposed in no way compromised his faith.[7] Paul Vallely, a Roman Catholic journalist writing in the *Church Times*, echoed Lord Winston in deploring the tone of much of the comment by the bishops – who were joined subsequently by several Anglican bishops.[8] He also drew attention to the poor understanding of the science that the clergy were showing:

> The idea that this violates a deep taboo, or destroys the concept of human uniqueness, or redefines what it is to be a human being, is predicated on the assumption that what is being created is an embryo.

This is why we hear talk about 'unborn human life', or even 'experiments on babies'. Yet using animal eggs to re-programme adult skin cells in a cellular cluster without a nervous system is not creating an embryo in any meaningful sense.[9]

But what startled many people was not just the Roman Catholic Church's carelessness about the science but the realization that there were MPs, including members of the Cabinet, who on the issue of this bill seemingly would not submit to the government whip but, in the name of 'informed conscience', would obey the 'Catholic whip' – as Paul Vallely called it. (In the event the government allowed its MPs to vote on the controversial clauses according to conscience, so we may never know whether or not they would have resigned, though even this concession was seen as the government bowing before pressure from the Roman Catholic hierarchy.) Letters to newspapers and comments on websites not only debated the substantive issue of the contents of the proposed legislation, but also the secondary matter of the role of religion in the public sphere. Opinion was divided, but a substantial number of people expressed anxiety that the Roman Catholic Church could exercise such influence over British legislators and seek to block progress in medical science in the name of religion. For a moment, there were echoes of nineteenth-century Britain before the Catholic Emancipation Act, when Roman Catholics were frequently regarded with suspicion if not as 'the enemy within'. Were the MPs' fundamental loyalties to the UK or to a creed and organization – the Roman Catholic Church – whose head office was based in Catholic Europe and which might not always have Britain's interest at heart?[10] This looked like a direct challenge to the British Parliamentary system whereby MPs are accountable not to any organization, religious or otherwise, but to their electors. The incident was possibly not in itself of the greatest significance, but it served to feed a growing perception that some people might have religious allegiances that transcended their loyalties to the British state and might even lead to conflicts of allegiance; and that fuelled an anxiety. But it is possible that people's real misgivings were not about Roman Catholicism, or not only about Roman Catholicism, but religion more widely. This issue involving Roman Catholics made people realize that there might be other faiths in the land that could exercise such a sway over their adherents. There was nervousness about where the loyalties of some believers might lie.

The row about Sharia

In fact, just before the row about the Human Fertilization and Embryology Bill another incident occurred, involving another Archbishop, that raised this very issue and produced a considerable reaction. This time the controversy was wholly unforeseen and caught everyone by surprise. It may even have coloured the subsequent reaction to Archbishop O'Brien's Easter sermon on the part of the liberal establishment.

In February 2008, the Archbishop of Canterbury gave a lecture to a group of lawyers at the Royal Courts of Justice.[11] The lecture was densely written and not easy to understand in either spoken or written form. It is possible that few journalists would have bothered to report it had not the Archbishop himself sought to give it, and the course of public lectures of which it was the first, some publicity by being interviewed on the BBC Radio 4's *World at One* programme. Dr Williams was concerned with the place of faith communities in Britain and wanted to find ways of making each feel rooted, valued and at home here. He noted that some religious communities already used traditional religious precepts to resolve issues in domestic and contractual matters. So he argued for the possibility of our paying respect to this 'custom and community' by accommodating some of these religious practices within British law. This was especially important where, without proper scrutiny, control of such practices might be dominated by 'primitivists' rather than properly trained authorities. Although he made passing references to such matters as Roman Catholic sensibilities over gay adoptions and Jewish divorce, he devoted most of his speech to the idea of making 'accommodations' for Islamic Sharia law. He did not specify what or how but did say in his interview that such accommodations were 'unavoidable'. Many took him to mean that he was calling for a parallel legal system for family and some contractual matters based on Sharia to be allowed to exist alongside British law – though he denied this.

What Dr Williams appeared to have had in mind was the way in which some Pakistani Muslim communities with backgrounds in rural Kashmir (Mirpur) have continued the tradition of settling certain kinds of issues at the level of the local tribe (the *biradari* or brotherhood) rather than the state. This includes some issues around contracts but also questions of marriage and divorce. Marriage, for example, is arranged within the *biradari* by parents. Young people may object to a chosen partner but there will be strong pressure to accept the bride or groom chosen for them. Allowing young people to marry for love could not be countenanced – it could weaken extended family ties – and would result in a loss of honour (*izzat*). In some areas of Pakistan loss of honour can only be recovered by killing those who offend – something that we now know has extended to the UK as well.

Most non-Muslims would have little or no experience of Sharia, but they would know about some of the more extreme punishments meted out in some Muslim countries – amputations and beheadings – and they would know about honour killings. It was probably this that caused such a sharp reaction against what the Archbishop said, not least from some Muslim women.

In fact, all democracies already permit some flexibility in what they demand of their citizens for the benefit of minority groups, religious and otherwise, and for the sake of community cohesion. In the USA, Amish children are not required to attend school after the eighth grade but go to join their families on the farm. In the UK, financial regulations are relaxed to allow Islamic banks to offer mortgages in accordance with Sharia – which forbids interest payments. Both countries enable conscientious objectors to opt out of military service; and so on. But all of these are exceptions to what is the norm, and many of them – such as the 'rights of conscience' for Roman Catholic doctors not to undertake abortions – are only possible because they are rare. (If large numbers of social workers refused to process adoptions for gay couples injustices would arise.) If this were all the Archbishop was advocating it is hard to see why he devoted an entire lecture asking for what already happens. But if he were suggesting something more – for some people in some parts of the country to (voluntarily) live under Sharia law and Sharia courts – this was something very different; it was asking not for a few exceptions from the norm but the creation of alternative norms. Since this was not clarified, no one, certainly not the Archbishop, addressed all the practical questions that immediately arise. There are, for instance, many versions of Sharia – in fact six principal schools of Sunni and Shi'ite law. Which version would prevail? What would happen when those who submitted to Sharia came into conflict with those who did not? Whose norms would then prevail?[12] There is also what we might call – after Tam Dalyell's famous West Lothian Question – the 'Sparkbrook Question' (after the Birmingham ward of Sparkbrook, which has a mainly Asian population): should those who submit to Sharia law be allowed to make laws for the rest of us? Many of the criticisms of the speech arose precisely because what David Aaronovitch called its 'direction of travel' was not made clear – what exactly it would look like in practice.[13]

Again, what concerns me here is not so much what the Archbishop was or was not advocating, but the public reaction to what people thought he was advocating. The interview and the subsequent reporting of the lecture had an immediate and incendiary effect – the Archbishop provoked hostility across the entire political and journalistic spectrum. The *Sun*'s headline, 'What a Burkha', was perhaps the most memorable as well as the rudest. But no more polite were those broadsheet writers who would normally give the Archbishop a sympathetic hearing. Ruth Gledhill, *The Times*' religion correspondent, asked in an online article, 'Has the Archbishop gone bonkers?' The columnist Matthew Parris headed his piece in the same newspaper, 'Williams is dangerous. He must be resisted.' Many Muslims were also quick to distance themselves from what the Archbishop said or was thought to have said. Yasmin Alibhai-Brown, writing in the *Independent*, said:

> What he did on Thursday was to convince other Britons, white, black and brown, that Muslims want not equality but exceptionalism and their own domains. Enlightened British Muslims quail. Friends like this churchman do us more harm than our many enemies. He passes round what he believes to be the benign libation of tolerance. It is laced with arsenic.[14]

Although Dr Williams had been careful to make clear that there would have to be resistance to the more inhumane practices of Sharia that conflicted with fundamental human rights, such as stoning adulterers and amputating the limbs of petty thieves, this did not stop some in the media speaking about Sharia in just these terms. Some of the reactions were probably – as the Archbishop's defenders claimed – simple Islamophobia, but many were thoughtful and careful responses. A hostile editorial in the *Daily Telegraph* concluded by saying:

> There are two quite separate points of legitimate concern. One is that the Archbishop – who heads a national institution with a constitutional function – explicitly called into question the most fundamental principle of British justice: that we have a single system of law that applies equally to everyone. The other is that, at a time when British cultural assumptions and institutions are under threat from a particularly aggressive interpretation of Islam, the head of the Established Church is unprepared to offer a robust defence of its values, apparently preferring to concede to the demands of what is in fact a minority, even among the Muslim community. Dr Williams is guilty, at the very least, of arrogant insensitivity. His self-inflicted injury may yet prove to be fatal.[15]

The Archbishop and his spokespersons sought to back away from what he had apparently advocated by saying that his remarks had been 'taken out of context' or 'misinterpreted', and he subsequently apologized to the Anglican Church's General Synod for any 'misleading choice of words' or 'unclarity'. But whatever the Archbishop actually said or meant by what he said, many people in the country clearly believed that what he was represented as advocating – that Muslims should be able to regulate some aspects of their life according to Sharia – was what many in the Muslim community wanted and were actively working towards. For every Muslim spokesman who said this was not what Muslims wanted, the reporters and broadcasters always found another who said the opposite. One imam was widely reported as saying that even some of the more savage aspects of Sharia might have a salutary and beneficial effect on the nation's morality. The ghost of Enoch Powell came into view again.

The uproar ran for several days. It seemed to bring to a head fears and anxieties that many people had been harbouring for a long time, principally about Islam but also about the place of religion in contemporary society more generally. Just before the row over Sharia there had been a row over adoption. The Roman Catholic Church's adoption agencies wanted to be able to receive state funding while also being able to refuse adoptions for prospective parents who were gay. How far should any religious body be allowed to plead conscience and a special case when public money was involved? As far as Islam was concerned, many felt that if Muslim communities were allowed to practise Sharia law with Sharia courts, the freedoms of many British Muslims would be put at risk. It is easy to say that Muslims could opt out of Sharia if they wanted to, but communities put pressure on individuals to conform: that, in an important sense, is what community is about. It is why, as a young person, I determined to escape – through education – from a working-class community whose norms I found stifling. The journalist Matthew Parris summed up this argument in this way:

> A Britain in which Muslim communities policed themselves would be ruthlessly policed, and probably more law-abiding than today. But it would be a Britain in which the individual Muslim – maybe female, maybe ambitious, maybe gay, maybe a religious doubter – would lose their chances of rescue from his or her family or community by the State. The State, not family, faith or community is the guarantor of personal liberty and intellectual freedom, and it will always be to the State, not the Church, synagogue or mosque, that the oppressed individual needs look.[16]

Similar points were made by Maryam Namazie, who founded the Council of Ex-Muslims. Sharia 'is fundamentally discriminatory and misogynist', and the idea that people could choose between Sharia and civil jurisdiction was flawed. Women would be coerced into accepting the Sharia court, and 'this would hit the people who need the protection of British law more than anyone else'.[17]

What Dr Williams had enabled many people to be very clear about was that not all religions are a version of the Archbishop's own liberal Anglicanism. What Matthew Parris draws attention to is that allowing any individuals within the nation state to have their legal rights and entitlements determined by a religious membership rather than as a result of citizenship would be to betray everything the people of Britain had struggled for over several centuries; for one of the achievements of the modern state is that it privileges individual rights over those of communities, even sacred communities.

There is no doubt that the row about Sharia reinforced the belief of many people in Britain that some religions, if not all, posed a real threat to the rights of some individuals and to community cohesion, and needed careful monitoring and perhaps restraining. The wisdom of the government's policy of engaging with faith groups somewhat indiscriminately began to look questionable.

Islamist extremism

But the deepest anxieties about the role of religion in British society and its potential for causing division came as a result of the series of terrorist attacks and foiled terrorist attempts from July 2005. Until that time it is probably true to say that few people had much understanding of Islamic extremism, and even those who had were not sure that it was likely to impact significantly on the UK. Now we know. Since that date the government, police and the intelligence services have made strenuous efforts to discover as much as possible in as short a time as possible.

Islamic extremism is essentially a legacy of the encounter between the more traditional world of Islam and the rapidly modernizing world of the West, the symbolic beginning of which was Napoleon's invasion of Egypt in 1798. For the next two centuries the proud and ancient civilization of Islam was overwhelmed by the military and economic power of European nations. Thoughtful Muslims began a period of soul-searching as they sought to discover the secret of Europe's success. In 1846, for example, Muhammad al-Saffar, a high-ranking Muslim official in Morocco, was part of a delegation invited to Paris by King Louis-Philippe I. He was bowled over by France's military capability, its conduct of affairs, its legal system. What was the secret? He wrote that the French:

> are not content with knowing things by tradition, but study the roots of a matter (before) drawing conclusions. Only then do they decide whether to accept or reject it. If a craftsman does something (new), his prestige and reputation are increased. Then the state rewards him, praises him and makes much of him. In that way the desire for progress is cultivated among them.[18]

Questioning, flexibility and innovation – these were the keys to success in every sphere. But the fear was that Islam had bequeathed a cultural legacy that was simply too static to respond positively to modernity. Central to Islamic societies is the Qur'an, which Muslims of all schools accept as the very speech of God – this is why the memorizing of Qur'anic verses is at the heart of all Islamic study. The believer approaches the scriptures in some fear and trembling. For a Muslim, it is brave to interrogate, impious to challenge, yet impossible to ignore the Qur'an. Ernest Gellner wrote that 'Christianity has its Bible belt; Islam is a Qur'an belt.'[19] As a result, Islam sets great store by *taqlid* – reliance on what is held to be unchanging tradition – rather than *ijtihad* – exercising independent judgement to arrive at fresh interpretations. All of this encourages a conservative rather than an innovative stance towards the world.

Al-Saffar did not see any particular relationship between the European culture of intellectual flexibility and Christianity since he did not believe the French were particularly religious. He found 'infidelity (*kufruhum*) and the extinction of the light of religion from their hearts'.[20] Perhaps as a Muslim he did not want to find any such relationship. In fact Christianity, especially in its Protestant form, had learnt both the necessity for change and the means of assimilating it – that willingness to entertain the possibility of new ideas that rightly impressed those nineteenth-century Muslim observers. But for whatever reason, Muslim societies did not find it easy to accommodate themselves to Western modernity. A 'Protestant Islam' did not develop. But as the West intruded more and more on most of the Islamic world through colonial expansion across Africa, the Near East and South Asia, 'westoxification' – a star-struck admiration of the West – increasingly gave way to resentment. There began to grow a yearning for renewal. Some wanted a simple return to traditional ways; others believed that aspects of modernity could be employed in the service of an alternative Islamic system – a *nizam*. These were the Islamists. They also believed that the new or renewed Islamic system could only be achieved through struggle – *jihad*.

It is a mistake to think of Islamic extremists as wanting a return to some Medieval past. What they want is to use the power of the modern state for the benefit of the ordinary Muslim. This is why they resent most of the existing Muslim regimes – the monarchies of Saudi Arabia and Jordan, the military dictatorships that have ruled from time to time in Pakistan, and the more secular governments of Egypt and Turkey – as well as Western governments. It is also why they despise most of those responsible for running local mosques.

Islamist movements began in Egypt with the founding of the Muslim Brotherhood by Hassan Al-Banna in 1928, and in Pakistan with the Jamaat-e Islam (Islamic society) in 1941, led by Mawlana Mawdudi. The real expansion came after 1966, when the intellectual leader of the Brotherhood in Egypt, Sayyid Qutb, was hanged and many extremists fled to other Muslim nations. This turned him into a martyr. Since then Islamist groups proliferated across the Muslim world, and by the 1970s were a force everywhere. Qutb wrote a number of books that gave the movement its key ideas about the social and political role of Islam.[21] (All of this, of course, predates the wars in Iraq and Afghanistan, which at one time were regularly presented as the reason for Muslim extremism. British and American foreign policy may be the latest example of the infidel's hatred of Islam and, therefore, the latest excuse for violence, but they are not the cause of Islamic extremism.)

It was, however, in Iran in 1979 that the decisive break with the Western, secular version of the modern state was made. The Iranian revolution brought to power the Shi'ite cleric Ayatollah Khomeini who, even after his death in 1989, continues to inspire all Muslims, whether Sunni or Shia. Khomeini's victory was of enormous symbolic importance. It showed that the dream of a modern Islamic state, able to take on and defeat the West, especially the Great Satan, the USA, was not an impossible one. The young men who blew themselves up on the London transport system dreamed this dream; they were part of this movement. Their allegiance was not to their country; Islamists do not really have national allegiances. The dream is not of a series of separate Islamic states – often the legacy of colonialism – but of one Islamic community, the *umma*, stretching across the Muslim world and gradually drawing into itself the non-Islamic world as well. This is the political-theological vision that motivates the extremists and is the reason why if it is to be defeated it must in part be defeated by theology. Those who are attracted need to hear alternative theological arguments to those of the Islamic movement.

After July 2005, the people of the UK realized they had in their midst some who had a particular interpretation of their religion that led them to commit terrorist acts, not in some distant country but against their own country and their fellow citizens. It was a profoundly disturbing moment. But it raised in the most acute form the

87

question of religion and cohesion. It raised it, moreover, in a very particular way. The question was not so much whether there was something about religion in general that threatened cohesion – as the secularists were saying – as whether there was something about this particular religion, Islam, that lent itself or gave rise to a more intolerant and anti-integrative stance in society. Richard Dawkins might think that all religions were as bad as one another, but many other people were not convinced. We must now take this argument head on.

When I talk to Muslim friends about the presence of Islamists in their mosques, it calls to mind some painful memories of my own from the 1970s and 1980s. These are political memories of attempts by radical political groups – the Militant Tendency, Socialist Organizer – to take power in the Labour Party. This is not comparable in all respects to what we find with radical Islam, but some comparison may provide insights. The techniques used by members of these groups were not dissimilar to the techniques used by Islamists now. The Labour Party militants had three goals: to infiltrate the party; befriend and win recruits among the younger membership; and destabilize the existing leadership. At different times I was a Labour Party constituency party officer, a ward councillor and Deputy Leader of a metropolitan district council – a prime target. They also had a powerful narrative – a form of Marxism – to explain society's problems and guide future action. Whatever the issue – problems with manufacturing industry at home or tension abroad – they had an analysis and a solution. They persuaded young minds that they were part of socialism's advance guard – and young people were flattered and exhilarated to believe they had been recruited to play such an important role. Many in the party – Tony Benn comes to mind – defended their right to express their views but turned a blind eye to their intimidatory conduct. Their most persuasive attribute was their certainty. They knew what socialism was and what had to be done. One of their greatest weapons was to suggest that others were not proper socialists. As a councillor, I had to take political decisions that involved compromise and the art of the possible – taking into account available resources, making allowance for other points of view and so on. This was represented as weakness and bad faith. Moreover, they were tireless in their pursuit of their goals, not least because

outside work they had no other life. For many, the small core of political radicals was a substitute family, a network of support. They lived
for politics.

Similarly, as Ed Husain, Shiv Malik and Hassan Butt have docu-
mented, Islamists target and befriend younger Muslims, gradually
winning their confidence and introducing them to the ideas of such
radicals as Qutb and Mawdudi.[22] In the case of young Muslims, what
makes them so vulnerable is that they are approached at a point in
their lives where they are struggling with the question of identity –
a recurring theme in these chapters. Hassan Butt has said how as a
young man he felt neither British nor Pakistani:

> When I went to Pakistan I was rejected. And when I came back to
> Britain, I never felt like I fitted in to the wider British community. And
> you've got to remember that a lot of our parents didn't want us to fit
> in to the British community.[23]

This is a dilemma for the second generation of all immigrant
groups; it is made more difficult where the migrant community is so
different from the host community in so many ways – skin-colour,
culture, religion. What the Islamists offer is a way to ease the tension. The route to salvation is to see yourself as neither British nor
Pakistani but Muslim (in some transnational sense), part of the
purified community of political Islam. As Butt says: 'You can be
anywhere in the world and this identity will stick with you and give
you a sense of belonging.'[24]

This enables young Muslims to see themselves as good Muslims,
without having to adopt all the attitudes and customs of their parents. It also allows them to deal with one of the most contentious
issues for the community: the question of marriage. Many young
British-born Muslim men do not want to marry within the *biradari*,
which often means marrying a 'cousin' from Pakistan. But the
Islamists take the view that Muslims should not be divided by
either tribalism or nationalism, therefore a Muslim is free to
marry a pious Muslim who is not a family member (as Mohammad
Sidique Khan did), making it possible to marry for love. In so far
as the older generation or more traditionally minded Muslims
seek to impose the customs of Pakistan on the young, which are
often resented, they inadvertently drive them into the hands of the
Islamist extremists.

Mohammad Sidique Khan, who masterminded the London bombings, had previously tried to recruit other young Muslims to the *jihadi* cause in Manchester in 2001, where he had worked with Omar Sharif and Asif Hanif, who went on to commit terrorist outrages in Israel. The technique is to sympathize with young people's tensions and discontents, especially those caused by crises of identity, and seek to turn them against the leaders of the local mosques by suggesting that they do not understand because they are not proper Muslims. It is true that local leaders are often quite out of touch with younger people. In Khan's case, the leaders at his local mosque spoke and wrote in Urdu, and the only time they met younger attenders was when teaching the Qur'an – by rote, in Arabic. Above all the extremists have a narrative that they repeat with absolute conviction – a theological-political explanation for why things are as they are, what Allah wants for the future and how they can be not just a small part of that but a key part, as the advance guard. For those who are caught up with an extremist group, because these are the only people with whom they can share their thoughts on Islam and politics, the group 'becomes your family. It becomes your backbone and support.'[25]

For a few, there will be the temptation to become involved in 'offensive' *jihad* and in so doing make a considerable mark on the world of the infidel – an appeal to ultimate vanity. This part of the radicalization will almost certainly involve taking people out of their local context and probably out of the British context altogether – at one time to Afghanistan or to Syria or Pakistan – for more intensive training, especially in bomb-making techniques. They may continue to live with their family, maintain their job and outwardly seem little different. But inwardly they gradually withdraw mentally and emotionally into a bubble of extremist religious thought. They live for radical Islam.

One final feature of Islamism is its capacity to deal with people who have a history of living an un-Islamic life but want to change. The more traditional Muslim finds people with a past difficult to handle – they shame family and community. Islamists are not interested in what people may have done in the past but only what they are prepared to contribute in the future. Shiv Malik sums up his understanding of what motivated Mohammad Sidique Khan in this way:

Khan may have felt indignant about Western foreign policy, as many anti-war campaigners do, but that wasn't the reason he led a cell of young men to kill themselves and 52 London commuters. At the heart of this tragedy is a conflict between first and second generations of British Pakistanis – with many young people using Islamism as a kind of liberation theology to assert their right to choose how to live. It is a conflict between tradition and individuality, culture and religion, tribalism and universalism, passivity and action.[26]

Do experiences of struggle against militants in the Labour Party of the 1970s and 1980s give some pointers to how Islamism may be overcome? It must be said at once that the Labour Party political extremists were not easily and not instantly defeated, but nonetheless what lessons would I draw?

First, the general membership needs educating. They need to understand and accept what is happening. Too many in the Labour Party in the early days would not admit what was going on around them and made excuses. Then, second, fear has to be acknowledged and faced. Many Labour Party members allowed themselves to be intimidated by small groups of determined and sometimes unpleasant people. Third, respected leaders must be unequivocal in exposing and denouncing the extremists. For the Labour Party, a critical moment was the 1985 annual conference. Militant members had effectively insinuated themselves into the Labour Group of Liverpool City Council and had made the city almost ungovernable. The party leader, Neil Kinnock, made a speech pointing out the folly of Militant's philosophy and conduct, famously saying at one point:

I'll tell you what happens with impossible promises. You start with far fetched resolutions. They are then pickled into a rigid dogma, a code, and you go through the years sticking to that, out-dated, misplaced, irrelevant to the real needs, and you end in the grotesque chaos of a Labour council – a Labour council – hiring taxis to scuttle round a city handing out redundancy notices to its own workers.

The speech was courageous. It did not endear him to many party activists who were in a state of denial about the nature of the threat, and he had to be re-elected as party leader. He was reviled by many and called a traitor by some. It is not easy to admit publicly that an organization to which you are committed has such a major problem, especially when there are elections to fight. Kinnock's speech gave fresh heart to ordinary Labour Party members. It enabled them to face down the extremists in their ward parties because they now realized that the extremist narrative was false, that they were not alone, that others felt as they did and that they would be supported.

Islamic extremism, similarly, will only be defeated when Muslims first admit there is a problem among some of their own community. Hassan Butt, for instance, has written about a continuing willingness to believe that the July 2005 bombs were planted by British intelligence or the Israeli secret service, Mossad, rather than Muslims:

> Two years on [from the London bombings] I still hear the same conspiracy theories being clung to by a Muslim community that is living in a comforting state of denial.[27]

Butt thinks the culture of denial is 'deeply embedded' and that Muslims are 'burying their heads in the sand'. In part this is because the older generation, who emigrated here 'aspiring to work hard and to better their standard of living', were always 'law-abiding citizens whose loyalties lay with Britain in the main'. Muslim terrorism carries with it great shame for any families or communities implicated – Shiv Malik has written of the incomprehension and shame felt by the parents of the 7 July bombers.[28] But for some Muslims, even if Muslim extremism is acknowledged, the attitude towards it may be ambiguous: is it not understandable or even justified given what is happening to Muslims across the world? If those who are opposed to terrorism nevertheless find themselves conflicted in this way, they will never give the clear lead necessary for steering impressionable young people away from extremism.

Part of overcoming the denial consists in understanding what is happening to Islam worldwide and why it is proving such a struggle for Muslims to come to terms with the modern world. As part of that, key passages in the Qur'an have to be faced – such as those texts relating to the treatment (including the killing) of non-Muslims. Butt believes there is a reluctance to admit that such texts even exist. Islam, it is said, is a religion of peace. This is dangerous because it plays into the hands of the extremists who accuse local leaders of telling untruths about the Qur'an – and they point to the relevant passages to prove the point. Similarly with the concept of *jihad*, the struggle against unbelief but also unbelievers: this is causing serious problems and needs careful explanation theologically, setting the texts in context. There is a considerable responsibility for Muslim scholars in the West to do this necessary work since there is little being done elsewhere in the Muslim world. Meanwhile, on countless websites and in the easily available books and pamphlets of the exponents of political Islam, young minds are being fed by a depressing diet of radical sentiment.

Then there must be a willingness on the part of more Muslims to take greater responsibility for what happens in their mosques, not least because the current leaderships may need support. There is intimidation, as Ed Husain has made clear. Above all, the Muslim community needs to think through what it means to be British and Muslim, and to do this it needs help from Muslim theologians and writers. There is a great deal of literature in mosques and bookshops inviting Muslims to see the world through the eyes of the extremists; there is very little that sets out to give a coherent account of how one can be a good Muslim and a good citizen of a non-Muslim state. Hassan Butt says something similar:

> What Muslims need to do is go back to our books: we need to debate the teachings that are used to radicalize young men and legitimate the killing of innocent people. We need to discuss and refashion the set rules that govern how Muslims – whose homes and souls are planted firmly in the West – live alongside non-Muslims.

Militant and other groups were eventually rooted out of the Labour Party, but only after many years and only after effort on all fronts: facing the truth about Militant and being prepared to expose its intimidatory presence; setting out a coherent political narrative for democratic politics; being aware that young people were being recruited; accepting responsibility within the organization; and so on. Similarly, within the British Muslim community an effort on all fronts is necessary, beginning with an honest facing of the truth: there is a contemporary version of political Islam that holds allure for many young minds.

Summary and conclusion

In each chapter of this book we have been considering the question, 'Does religion undermine social or community cohesion?' from a variety of different perspectives. I have tried to suggest that there is no 'Yes' or 'No' answer but something more complex. There are situations in which religion and religious communities can be a source of bonding and bridging capital and play a constructive role in making communities cohesive. It would be foolish of government not to recognize and support that – it is in the national interest. In this chapter I have tried to illustrate situations in which religion and religious communities can undermine or threaten social or community cohesion. In the more serious instances of that, such as the request for a parallel religious legal system or the growth and presence of religious extremism, the state must act. If it does not, local communities are divided against themselves – as is the nation as a whole.

But is there not a sense in which the very presence of any religion that makes exclusive claims to sacred and ultimate truths is a threat to cohesion in a plural society? This will be considered in the final chapter.

5

Faith's ambiguous presence

————◆•◆————

> Your Christ is Jewish
> Your car is Japanese
> Your pizza is Italian
> Your democracy is Greek
> Your coffee is Brazilian
> Your holiday is in Turkey
> Your numbering is Arabic
> Your writing is Latin
> So is your neighbour a foreigner?
> *Graffito*[1]

> We want people of all backgrounds to feel confident about their identity and to have respect for other people's identity, within a positive, inclusive sense of Britishness, underpinned by values that we all share.[2]   *David Blunkett MP, Home Secretary, 2004*

> Multiculturalism has seemed to imply, wrongly for me: let other cultures be allowed to express themselves but do not let the majority culture at all tell us its glories, its struggles, its joys, its pains.
> *John Sentamu, Archbishop of York, 2005*

What I have argued throughout these chapters is that the question, 'Does religion help or hinder community cohesion?' is not one that can be answered in general terms; context and circumstance are everything. Those who say religion is always a force for good and those who say religion is toxic are equally guilty of being too sweeping in their assessment. Religion plays different roles in different social contexts, as I have sought to illustrate. But a more general argument is also made from time to time, to the effect that because a revealed religion (such as Christianity and Islam) lays exclusive claim to know the mind or will of God, and either explicitly or implicitly denies the claims of others, it is always going to be a

95

destabilizing force in a religiously plural society. The philosopher Stuart Hampshire summed it up in this way: 'Obviously, if one God, only one morality – His law and the falsity of moral pluralism therefore.'[3] This general argument also needs to be examined and I will do so in this final chapter.

But first, I want to begin to draw the threads of the discussion together by reflecting further on what kind of cohesive society we want and can realistically hope for given the nature of contemporary Britain as a multifaith, multicultural and multiethnic society; and what the contribution of religion could be given possible developments over the next few years. Will the positive contribution of religion outweigh anything negative? Can anything be done to eliminate the negative and accentuate the positive? The discussion here will be a mix of the empirical (what we already know), the speculative (what seems most likely) and the evaluative (what I think is most desirable). I will begin with the question of cohesion.

Measuring cohesion

How does the government measure community cohesion? It does so in part by asking questions through the Citizenship Survey – such as, 'To what extent do you agree or disagree that this local area (within 15/20 minutes walk) is a place where people from different backgrounds get on well together?'[4] Altogether, the government uses six indicators of cohesion:

- the percentage of people who believe people from different backgrounds get on well together in their local area;
- the percentage of people who have meaningful interactions with people from different backgrounds;
- the percentage of people who feel they belong to their neighbourhood;
- the percentage of people who feel they can influence decisions in their locality;
- whether there is a thriving third sector (voluntary bodies);
- the percentage of people who participate in culture or sport.

On the whole the evidence is encouraging. According to the 2005 survey, 80 per cent of British people were positive about their local communities. The 2007 survey confirms this: 81 per cent said people from different backgrounds got on well together in their area; in addition, 85 per cent of people said they felt strongly that they were British; and 77 per cent said they felt strongly that they belonged to their neighbourhood.[5]

However, a rather different picture emerges if different questions are posed. For instance, in 2008 the BBC commissioned a survey to mark the fortieth anniversary of Enoch Powell's 'Rivers of blood' speech around the issue of immigration. This revealed that six out of ten people thought there were too many immigrants in the country; three-quarters said immigration was causing tensions; and two-thirds believed it would lead to violence. On the other hand, the poll revealed that the number of people confessing to being racially prejudiced had fallen from 24 per cent in 2005 to 20 per cent in 2008.[6]

The evidence from the Burnley Project (discussed in Chapter 3) from those North-West towns where communities are often fairly sharply divided along ethnic and religious lines also paints a more mixed picture. The Asian young people surveyed displayed attitudes that were generally tolerant and integrative. Being religious themselves, they saw value in the religion of others. But the white working-class enclaves were relatively untouched by religion, and the attitude of a substantial minority of young people there to faith – any faith – was hostile. They did not see any value in other cultures – a rejection, in other words, of multiculturalism, which has been the prevailing political orthodoxy.

We need to understand the lessons of these conflicting pieces of evidence. Clearly, a great deal depends on the question that is asked. Much also turns on what issues are making headlines at the time of asking. In 2008, immigration became front-page news again not least because of pressures on local-authority services in areas of high immigration and high-profile crimes involving immigrants – a gruesome murder in Scotland of a Lithuanian woman, and revelations about trafficking and arms smuggling. These concerns have given further impetus to the government's overall approach, which is to pursue policies of community cohesion.

For and against multiculturalism

Until recently, however, 'multiculturalism' rather than 'community cohesion' has been the term used to encapsulate how we think

society should be ordered in the UK in the face of a growing pluralism. Multiculturalism has shaped the broad strategic direction of
public policy, so why is it now being judged and found wanting,
giving way to community cohesion? After all, it is not so long since
any criticism of multiculturalism was viewed (at least on the political left and in most religious circles) as little more than disguised
racism; public debate around the idea was then impossible. But now
multiculturalism has all but lost its politically correct status and is
the subject of lively debate.[7]

Since there are many definitions of multiculturalism, let me
suggest what I think it came to mean in the British context as far
as the public authorities were concerned. The term came into use
in response to the large-scale, post-war immigration throughout
Europe of ethnic and religious groups whose religion and culture
were very different from that of the host communities. In the UK,
after the (largely Christian) Afro-Caribbean immigration, the majority of newcomers were from Asia and the predominant faith was
Muslim. In policy terms, multiculturalism was an attempt to make
welcome and affirm these new arrivals by valuing and supporting
their different religions and cultures. Although he did not call the
government's approach 'multiculturalism' but 'integration', we can
see the beginning of the multiculturalist approach in these words
of Roy Jenkins, Home Secretary, in 1966:

> I define integration, therefore, not as a flattening process, but as equal
> opportunity accompanied by cultural diversity in an atmosphere of
> mutual tolerance. This is the goal . . . [If] we are to maintain any sort
> of world reputation for civilized living and social cohesion, we must
> get far nearer to its achievement than is the case today.[8]

Mass immigration was making a substantial and permanent difference to the country; Britain was ceasing to be a homogeneous
society and was becoming culturally very diverse. There was a de-
liberate turning away from what was seen as the destructive and
narrow ethno-religious nationalisms that had so often disfigured
Europe in the past. Affirmation included supporting minority
languages; teaching about other faiths in the religious education
syllabus; celebrating the festivals of other faiths publicly, such as
Diwali and Eid; discriminating positively in public appointment

and representation to ensure a fair balance of people from minority cultures; allowing distinctive dress of other faiths in schools and the workplace; encouraging the arts and music of minority cultures; and so on. British multiculturalism was in some contrast to the approach in France, where the stress was on French culture, and religion was excluded from the public arena – *laïcité*. French schoolchildren, for example, were not allowed to wear distinctive religious adornment – such as the *hijab* or the Star of David – in the classroom.

It was never clear whether Britain's cultural pluralism was supposed to be a goal of public policy or the means of arriving at some other goal. Was it a stage on the way to a new cultural dispensation, after we had learnt from one another's cultures, or was it an attempt to freeze the country with the mosaic of cultures that it now had? This goes to the heart of the debate. Are we searching together for new forms of the common good for our time, ways of living together that bring out what is best from our respective cultures but move us all on to something new; or are we forever locked in our separate metaphorical or actual enclaves? If the former, then multiculturalism seems to me to be a good. It does not assume *ab initio* that another culture (and I include religion in this) is without merit or not worthy of consideration. However, in that case, as Zygmunt Bauman has said, 'recognition of cultural variety is the beginning, not the end, of the matter; it is but a starting point for a long and perhaps tortuous, but in the end beneficial, political process'.[9] Multiculturalism in practice, however, seemed to be the idea that cultural pluralism was good in itself.

The unspoken assumption of multiculturalism in that sense (cultural pluralism as an end in itself) was that all cultures were equally valuable, and all aspects of all cultures were equally valuable. As a result, we had no way of choosing between cultures, no means of preferring or prioritizing; no way of evaluating the music of an Aboriginal didgeridoo or a Mozart symphony. We could never say that in this respect this was better or richer or more worthwhile than that. (The same attitude guided the post-1960s teaching of religion in schools: all religions were placed on a par, with no means of discriminating between them.) Multiculturalism is cultural relativism and cultural relativism, while it promises tolerance, actually breeds indifference: if there is nothing to choose between cultures why bother with anyone else's? (The white young people of the urban enclaves had certainly learnt that lesson!) As a result, we became paralysed, unable to mount any criticism of minority cultures and fearful of 'imposing' anything of the dominant culture on others – hence the decisions of some local authorities to replace Christmas with Winterval and prohibit nativity plays in inner-city schools for fear of imposing something alien. Hence too the Archbishop of York's fear quoted at the head of this chapter, that every culture could express itself except that of the host community. No doubt part of the reason for this was post-imperial guilt; we did not want to treat other people and their cultures in Britain as we had once treated them when we were the colonial power.

This was the politically correct position until it began to collapse, partly under the weight of its own absurdities and partly as a result of a growing realization that there were some elements in other cultures that jarred with previously accepted British values. This realization was slow to come because multiculturalism had the effect of stifling critical debate. Relativism says everything is equally valuable; but if everything is equally valuable then that is only another way of saying that nothing is valuable, because for something to be valuable there must be a contrast with something that is not as valuable or not valuable at all.

Multiculturalism, therefore, as it developed had two lasting consequences. First, it affirmed the right of people to have their own cultures and to be different from the dominant culture. We learnt to practise tolerance, and that was good. But in the second place, we became indifferent towards other cultures. After all, if there is nothing to choose between them, there is no point in taking any of them seriously. Frank Furedi has expressed the same point trenchantly in a criticism of the country's intellectual leaders:

> The fraudulent project of treating diversity as an end in itself serves as an escape clause for an elite that lacks the capacity to believe in a clearly formulated moral purpose.[10]

By a different route we arrived at almost the same place as those who assert the superiority of their own culture while knowing little and caring less about that of others. I say almost because we also undermined and became indifferent to our own culture!

Core values of cohesive and plural societies

The idea of community cohesion (and we must remember that the government couples this with 'integration') has been developed in part as a reaction to these perceived failures and inadequacies of multiculturalism. In particular, the recognition that there might be conflict between the values of different minorities or between a minority group and the wider society has led to the conclusion that if society is to be cohesive there must be some core values that are shared by all. The debate, therefore, has shifted to consider what those values are. This is sometimes referred to as a search for 'Britishness', a search that often ends fruitlessly as people seek to describe what they think constitutes the essence of the British character or British way of life – and others disagree. It has certainly taken a number of people down some strange by-ways in recent years. Norman Tebbit, for example, when Chairman of the Conservative Party (1985–7), was widely derided for suggesting that the sign of successful integration would be when immigrant groups passed the 'cricket test': we could only regard people as integrated if they supported the English cricket team rather than the team of their family origins – Pakistan or India or the West Indies. John Major, as Prime Minister, thought that Britishness was all about 'long shadows on country cricket grounds, warm beer, invincible green suburbs, dog lovers and pools fillers and – as George Orwell said "old maids bicycling to holy communion through the morning mist"'.[11] Gordon Brown has also insisted on the need for 'Britishness' but has been less clear about what that might be.[12]

But is this search for common values around which the nation can cohere misleading and quite possibly destructive? So far it has been unproductive, principally because it ignores the fact that modern societies are dynamic and constantly evolving. In the Middle Ages a very large part of what it was to be 'British' (though to use this term before the Act of Union in 1707 is anachronistic) – to live in these islands – was to be religious and Catholic. After the Reformation the British were just as religious though now largely Protestant. But by the beginning of the twenty-first century a substantial number of people were not religious at all, though they were no less British. In other words, the values that even the majority of people in a given country embrace may change over time. In addition, as traditional authorities – church or state – lose the capacity or desire to impose religious beliefs or ethical norms on people, the range of possible values that people may choose to live by grows ever more diverse – though we should not underestimate how much we are influenced and shaped by the values of the cultures in which we are raised, even if we are not consciously claiming them as our own. We are not going to find, however, fixed values universally accepted as the basis for a cohesive society. In these circumstances we would be well advised to find a basis for our common life that assumes disagreement around values and not consensus. But there is always the danger that the search for Britishness might result in some set of values being identified and promoted. This would no doubt please some but it would deeply alienate others – as the attempt to write into the proposed European constitution something about Christian values alienated those who were either not Christian or not religious. The days of the homogenous nation state lie in the past. The search for Britishness is a distraction. The idea that cohesion requires a 'shared future vision' in this sense (part of the government's definition) is a mistake. It is like searching for the Holy Grail.

If cohesion does depend on a core of common values, they are not going to be values of this kind – religious beliefs, ethical norms. Indeed, the modern history of the UK – and the rest of Europe – has in large measure been the history of moving away from thinking that cohesion can only be achieved when people have shared values of this kind. That way led to the continental wars of religion – 'une foi, un loi, un roi' – and totalitarian political regimes, from revolutionary France to communist Russia, as those in authority sought to impose common values on all their citizens. Instead, we have come to realize that if a plurality of values is inevitable, cohesion has to be brought about by another route. In this way the liberal state gradually emerged as we struggled to work out what legal and constitutional arrangements were necessary for people with different values to live together in relative harmony. These 'contractual' arrangements are the 'core values' of the liberal state which, it is worth saying, are a large part of the reason that immigrants want to come here in the first place. If we want a cohesive society where there is maximum freedom for people to pursue those things that they believe are valuable and worthwhile, then we must all acquiesce in the following, which we can call the political values of the liberal state:

- respect for the rule of law;
- equality of all citizens before the law;
- democratically elected government;
- freedom of speech;
- freedom of assembly;
- freedom of worship;
- freedom of the individual to live their life as they wish subject only to not interfering with the rights of others;
- tolerance and respect for those who differ from us.

The point about the above is that we can all agree on them, whatever our religion, whatever our culture. Or rather, by acquiescing in them, we have no need to find cohesion through shared values, and that enables us to avoid both the frustration of a quest without a conclusion – the search for the Holy Grail – and the absurdity of trying to impose a particular set of values on everyone. These political values, or 'contractual' arrangements, are necessary if the community is to avoid the kind of repression that happens when societies seek to impose or engineer common values. If aspects of the culture of particular groups – ethnic or religious or both – conflict with them, then they must be rejected as inimical to what makes living together without undue coercion or repression possible. We would, of course, be open to challenges to these values – that, after all, is implicit in 'respect for others'. But if we cannot be persuaded, we would have to reject practices that came into conflict with them. So, for example, the refusal of divorce, or the subordination of women, or discrimination against people of a different gender, would all be incommensurable with these values of the liberal state.

These contractual arrangements and political values are common to all the nations of the Western world. But there is a way of speaking about them that captures the peculiarly British way of holding and experiencing them, and perhaps it takes an immigrant to appreciate just what that is. Isaiah Berlin (whose Jewish-Russian family emigrated here) once put it like this – and for 'English' I think we can read 'British':

> I cannot judge English values impartially, for they are part of me: I count this as the greatest of intellectual and political good fortune. These values are the basis of what I believe: that decent respect for others and the toleration of dissent are better than pride and a sense of national mission; that liberty may be incompatible with, and better than, too much efficiency; that pluralism and untidiness are, to those who value freedom, better than rigorous imposition of all-embracing systems, no matter how rational and disinterested, or than the rule of majorities against which there is no appeal. All this is deeply and uniquely English, and I freely admit that I am steeped in it, and believe in it, and cannot breathe freely save in a society where these values are for the most part taken for granted.[13]

What makes us British, as opposed to French or American, is then not so much those values, which most Western nations hold in common, but those values in the context of the history of our particular struggle to win them, the way we hold to them, and our affection for the land in which they were forged. This affection comes about 'naturally' through our being born here or out of a strong desire to make these values and the UK our own by choosing to live here, as Berlin's family chose to live here. This is why we found the attitudes of the July bombers almost incomprehensible. What had happened to them that they so came to hate the land that had nurtured them, the land that so many of their co-religionists were proud of or so anxious to be part of?

These values are not absolute. We may, for instance, have to forgo to some extent and for a time something of the freedom we enjoy in the interests of public safety or national security. In recent years, the threat of terrorism from the Provisional IRA and then Islamist extremists has led to lively debates about how much freedom we have to concede in order to remain safe – for example, in deciding how long the police may hold a suspect without charge.

If we return to the models of social organization and the continuum that I suggested in Chapter 1, we can see now that what I identified then as 'parallel lives' is simply the outworking of multiculturalism. The continuum could, therefore, be rewritten as:

Models of Social Organization:
Multiculturalism—Community cohesion—Assimilation

Both ends of the continuum are regarded as undesirable. We do not seek simple assimilation, for this would imply the destruction of minority cultures. Nor do we seek to affirm every aspect of the newer cultures that have migrated to Britain – multiculturalism. That would require us to value some aspects of cultures that we reject, and that would produce impossible tensions. (This was the anxiety thrown up by the row about Sharia that was discussed in Chapter 4.) Rather, the commitment to cohesion is a commitment to a journey together whereby we can be enriched with what is good and worthwhile in other cultures, but at the same time can challenge those aspects of other cultures that are alien to the core values of the liberal state. This is community cohesion as opposed to multicultur-alism and assimilation. But there are consequences for religion.

Social differentiation and Christianity

When we look at Britain today (as with every country in the West), we find organized religion having to respond and adapt to what sociologists call a socially differentiated society. In the undiffer-entiated society, religion was taken for granted, part of the air you breathed from the day you were born until the day you died; an individual did not have to make a decision for religion, he or she simply was religious; religion was the sacred canopy under which the totality of life was ordered and given meaning.[14] In a differenti-ated society – part of the process of secularization – religion is not taken for granted; the church is one voluntary body among many; and individuals have to make some decision, however minimal, for (or against) religion. Crucially, in the differentiated society, many aspects of life that were previously under the direct influence or control of organized religion – such as education, social order, justice, law – become autonomous.

This situation is one Christianity has been dealing with and thinking about for a long time. Islam has less experience of differ-entiation – something to which we must return. The fracturing of the organic unity between church and society took place in the UK gradually over a period of about four centuries. Anthony Russell has charted some of the more recent history in a study of eighteenth- and nineteenth-century Anglican clergy.[15] The clergy that we see populating the novels of Jane Austen and Henry Fielding performed many roles in addition to being preachers and pastors – officer of law and order, schoolteacher, almoner, officer of health. We can get some feel for the more undifferentiated society from these remarks of the Church of England Bishop Richard Watson shortly after the French Revolution, when law and order was one of the functions of the local parson and the state scarcely had a role:

> The safety of every civil government is fundamentally dependent on the hopes and fears of another world which are entertained by its members; and the safety of every Christian civil government is brought into the most imminent danger, when infidelity is making rapid progress in the minds of people . . . It may be difficult to find a full remedy for this evil, but the residence of a respectable clergyman in every parish and hamlet in which there is a place of established worship, appears to me to be more fitted than any other for that purpose.[16]

But as the centuries passed, these roles were gradually lost as the functions became the concern of discrete professions with their own bodies of (secular) knowledge, expertise, discipline and regulation, until only those of preacher, pastor and celebrant of the sacraments remained. Today, many Christians might want to argue that these lost roles were never the proper functions of the clergy in any case, and they should never have been involved in them; but that misses the point, which is that in the differentiated society organized religion loses its hegemonic control. In fact, during the twentieth century even the pastoral functions were lost as the welfare state expanded and new professionals came into existence – social workers, community workers, psychotherapists and counsellors.[17] The clergy faced a triple blow. As well as losing roles, the functions that remained to them in the more secular society – preacher and celebrant of the sacraments – ceased to have much social value. At the same time, under the influence of the Romantic movement, spirituality itself lost its exclusive anchorage in organized religion, so that the Church and the clergy were not necessarily valued even for their spiritual knowledge or expertise.

The Christian churches in the West have been learning, not without pain, to come to terms with these changes. In the UK, the transition has been from having almost monopolistic control over every aspect of the life of society to seeking to influence, recognizing that the churches are now in something of a religious and spiritual market place, competing with others. They have responded in one of two ways: either by seeking to (disinterestedly) serve the neighbourhood in which they are set – a 'community' model of the church – or by putting their main effort into drawing more individuals into active membership of their church – the 'gathered church' model. The two models are not mutually exclusive, but churches tend to be of one type or the other. The two models have produced two types of clergy. Those following a community model have incorporated into their ministries roles that the wider society does value – social worker, community worker, community development officer, counsellor. Others – the more evangelical – have turned away from the wider society and its concerns and have concentrated on those activities that build up congregational life – teaching, preaching and evangelizing. They are the ones who tend to have the growing congregations.

So, for example, many mainstream Christian churches, influenced by the community model, are committed to the areas in which they are situated. For the Anglican Church this has been a fairly natural progression, since it has always been organized territorially, with parishes and dioceses, and historically has taken the view that everyone living in the parish is a parishioner entitled to the benefits of 'membership' (though the Church of England has no test of membership). The tradition of attending the local parish church remains important for many Anglicans, despite the fact that the car makes it possible for them to go to more distant churches where they may find the style of worship more congenial. The local congregation is taught to have a concern for the geographical parish, to pray for its needs and to be involved in its life – part of the justification for continued establishment. Worshippers become governors of schools, trustees of local charities, committee members of good causes. Clergy may have chaplaincy roles in local hospitals and schools and will meet many others through their involvement in one or other of the occasional offices – baptisms, weddings and funerals. As we have seen, they will also have many and varied concerns beyond the parish. In some parts of the country where they are well-represented, Roman Catholic priests and Free Church ministers play similar roles. In other words, where churches once exercised a certain control over a parish and its parishioners, they may now have a community focus that will contribute much towards social capital in their localities and assist cohesion. This is the community model of church that government will have in mind when it seeks to involve the churches in its community cohesion agenda.

On the other hand, some more evangelical and Pentecostal churches may be less committed to a geographical area or not committed at all. Their churches could be anywhere. They are less community-orientated and more 'gathered' or 'associational'. Even so, they will teach their members to be responsible citizens and good neighbours. They also tend to be part of networks that draw people together across wider areas.

But both types of church – community or associational – understand that in Britain today the Christian church is a voluntary body, and individuals have to make some sort of decision to be part of it. Both models can assist social and community cohesion. There are exceptions: one or two smaller denominations resist as far as possible any engagement with the rest of society other than to see it as a recruiting ground – Jehovah's Witnesses, for example, will make friendships within the body of believers, disapprove of mixed marriages and refuse to allow members to take part in civil society; Witnesses do not vote or fight for Queen and country. In the USA, the Amish have taken this further by almost completely withdrawing into themselves.

In the light of this discussion we can also see why two of the incidents to which I referred in the last chapter – the intervention of Roman Catholic clergy over the Human Fertilization and Embryology Bill and the lecture given by the Archbishop of Canterbury on accommodating Sharia within British law – caused such an outcry in 2008. In both cases it seemed as if the clergy were trying to return the country to the position of the undifferentiated society in which, in the one case, the Church could directly influence parliament and, in the other, the interests of individuals were subordinated to those of religious bodies.

Differentiation and the Muslim community

We now need to contrast this experience of Christianity in Britain with that of Islam. Those Pakistani Muslims who migrated to Britain in the post-war period have moved from a relatively undifferentiated society in which religion is taken for granted and infuses every aspect of life, to one that is highly differentiated and in which religion is a matter of personal decision. In much of rural Pakistan the distinction we make between the religious and the secular spheres is relatively unknown – education, care of the sick, justice, social control, are all matters that fall under the direct influence of religion and religious authority. We can take one example, since it has become very contentious, and that is marriage.

Marriage, and particularly the role of women within marriage, has been intensively debated in the West for many decades. All the world's faiths have been accused of patriarchal and misogynistic attitudes. In the UK, marriage is regulated by the state and has been since the nineteenth century – and that offers women a certain protection. Marriages may be contracted in religious buildings and according to religious rites, but they have to conform to conditions laid down by the state, conditions that seek to safeguard the interests of the individual and not a religious body. For a marriage to be valid the parties must be over 18 (or 16 with parental permission); they must be uncoerced; and their intention must be that the marriage is for life. Each of these is important, not least for the position of women, especially very young women.

In rural Pakistan, marriage is religiously regulated and controlled. In the *biradari* system, marriages are arranged within the tribe. Marriage secures alliances within families and is a matter of honour. This is why many Pakistani young men and women find themselves making the journey to Pakistan to meet a cousin. In theory, bride and groom consent to the partners chosen for them; in practice the line between 'arranged' and 'forced' can be a thin one. There is growing evidence that some young people in the UK have been forced into marriages with Pakistani cousins to which they have not consented. Islam also allows men to marry girls as young as nine and to have up to four wives. Although forbidden in British law, some British Muslims have taken other wives and some argue for it as part of Sharia. There is no doubt that some Muslims would be happy to see a straightforward incorporation of these practices 'for Muslims' into British law. But this brings Sharia into conflict with British values and, therefore, poses a threat to cohesion.

It is important for Muslim women that British law and not Sharia governs marriage, as many of them have said. This outlaws forced marriages and offers protection for those who are married. The attempt by some Muslims to continue to treat marriage as they would in the undifferentiated society of Pakistan will inevitably produce tensions and strains in the differentiated countries of Western Europe and threaten cohesion.

British law is also an important safeguard against a practice among some Shia Muslims known as *muta*. The intention in marriage according to British law (and reflecting Christian values) is that it should be life-long. This contrasts sharply with *muta*, whereby marriages can be contracted for a very short period of time, even one night, in exchange for a fee rather than a dowry. Many Muslims find this equally shocking and see it as little more than licensed prostitution. British marriage law offers protection from that too.

These Islamic practices in other parts of the world are further reasons why the proposal by the Archbishop of Canterbury to incorporate parts of Sharia into British law (if that is what he said) was greeted with such alarm. It did much damage, since it gave the unfortunate impression that if Muslims keep up the pressure for Sharia, sooner or later a British government will give way – the Archbishop said it was 'inevitable'. But any continuing attempts by some members of the Muslim community to press for Sharia can only serve to erode the cohesiveness of communities.

The fundamental point of conflict between religion and the modern state is generally around issues of this kind – marriage, the place of women in society, homosexuality – all attempts to regulate the conduct of individuals. Organized religion requires to some degree conformity and obedience on the part of the worshipper. If that is voluntary there is no problem; but any attempt to impose practices more widely will be resisted. For this is what the differentiated society has rejected and it is this that lies at the heart of Western values around which Western societies cohere. The reason the suicide bombers did such damage to community cohesion was because in their renunciation of the land of their birth they revived the idea that the Muslim Asian minority were really outsiders whose interests were in perpetual conflict with those of the majority.

However, a substantial proportion, if not the majority, of British Muslims have no problem with the values that inform the British legal system as it relates to marriage. They are able to reconcile the refusal of polygamy with Qur'anic teaching without difficulty. Their argument is to set the Qur'anic passages in their historic context. The circumstance in which the Prophet permitted multiple marriage was that of caring for widows and their children when husbands were in short supply – usually due to war – and the economic status of women was precarious. The Prophet allowed men to take additional wives but made it clear that no man should contract a second or third marriage unless he could provide for each wife equally. The contemporary Muslim woman will insist that in the modern context this is not just a matter of material well-being but emotional and sexual too, and fulfilling those needs becomes impossible if there is more than one wife. The relevant text is:

> If ye fear that ye shall not be able to deal justly with the orphans, marry women of your choice, two or three or four; but if ye fear that ye shall not be able to deal justly (with them), then only one . . .   (Q4.3)

There is clearly a great deal of theological work of this kind to be done as Muslims learn how to live out their faith in the differentiated societies of the West.

When religion threatens cohesion

I have argued throughout these chapters that every dynamic and evolving society will face threats to its cohesion from time to time. There will always be legitimate issues that divide society, provoke passions and need addressing. When women were agitating for the vote; when the National Union of Mineworkers tried to stop pit closures; when many opposed the Iraq War, there were threats to cohesion. These are moments when the nation has to take stock and decide whether the discontents and the protests require change to public policy or have to be faced down. When a religious dimension is present the stakes can be much higher.

Social and community cohesion is threatened by religion in three ways. First, when a community feels under threat and emphasizes religion as a marker of its identity; second when people of faith, who may feel insecure for other reasons, believe the position or the honour of their religion is threatened; and third, and most seriously, when believers persuade themselves that they have some sort of divine mandate to forward their cause by any means, including violence. What can be done to minimize or manage these risks to social and community cohesion?

Religion and identity

Examples of the first threat – where religion is used to mark identity – can be seen in the recent history of the Balkans. When there were political and ethnic tensions, people who had lived in the same town all their lives suddenly saw themselves not as neighbours but as enemies, people of a different ethnicity and religion. The Serbs of Kosovo asserted their Orthodox Christianity when they felt pressure on their community from the majority Kosovan Albanians, who were Muslim. Although these were not really disputes about religion – the two faiths had existed side by side for generations – religious symbols, such as the cross and the crescent, became ethnic as well as religious symbols. Religion was co-opted to mark a clear boundary and reinforce a particular identity over against someone else. In Northern Ireland, the dispute between loyalists and nationalists – essentially a political dispute – was frequently badged as a dispute between 'Catholic' and 'Protestant', though it was not really a religious quarrel.

This mechanism is not always something to be deplored. In Eastern Europe, Christianity was used constructively towards the end of the Soviet period as a way of reminding a downtrodden people that they had once been a different people with a different way of looking at the world – and could be so again. As communism began to crumble, the churches were one of the few places where people could gather and explore alternatives; they were reminded of their Christian past. The particular context and circumstances make the difference. So in the UK we have seen the way in which extreme right-wing groups appropriate national symbols that have a religious connotation, such as the flag of St George, and patriotic hymns, such as 'Jerusalem', and may even invoke Christianity directly, especially when they want to oppose the (largely Muslim) Asian community. (The British National Party has recently changed tactics: anti-Semitism is now avoided and the Jews, who are white, are to be co-opted in the struggle of whites against Asians. Party spokespersons can now be heard defending 'Judaeo-Christian values' against Islamic.)

Although churchgoing may be low, the national census makes it clear that many people see themselves as 'Christians', which may in part be a way of identifying themselves as white; they are not of another religion associated with people of a different colour and ethnicity. Religion often lies dormant in a community until called upon to assist the maintenance of boundaries and the bolstering of identities, for good or ill. In other words, although we may not think that intracommunity tension could become a matter of religion in so-called secular Britain, experience elsewhere suggests it could. Risks to social and community cohesion in this way can be mitigated but probably not wholly overcome by churches (and public bodies) continuing to be clear that while British culture has been hugely shaped by Christianity, citizenship does not entail any particular religious identity.

Religion and honour

Turning to the second threat listed above, religion unsettles community cohesion when people of faith believe the integrity, the progress or the honour of their religion is at stake and that it is part of their religious duty to take action to 'defend' the faith. In these circumstances religion powerfully motivates and can supply justifications for illegal actions. In December 2004, for example, the Sikh community in the West Midlands took exception to a play, *Behzti*, at the Birmingham Repertory Theatre, which they believed portrayed their religion in a negative light. The play dealt with issues such as sexual abuse and honour killings. Some 400 Sikhs demonstrated outside the theatre; some broke down a foyer door and smashed equipment; three policemen were injured. Mohan Singh from the Guru Nanak Gurdwara in Birmingham thought that free speech could go too far and wondered whether it was worth upsetting several thousand Sikhs in Britain and millions elsewhere.[18] The Roman Catholic Archdiocese of Birmingham told its members to boycott the play. Few voices were heard from any religious quarter supporting the right and importance of the theatre to stage controversial plays without disruption. The theatre decided to cancel the run.

If one mark of a healthy democracy is a willingness to explore through drama topics that are uncomfortable within sections of the population, the inability or unwillingness of the community to defend the theatre was a set-back, an uncomfortable reminder of an earlier failure to be more robust in defending Salman Rushdie. It was a set-back too for religious groups in the eyes of the non-religious community, and so did damage to community relations. What the religious bodies failed to appreciate was that by using or supporting the threat of disruption they gave the impression (or may even have revealed) that they were not really committed to the liberal values of the democratic state but merely took advantage of them when it suited them. Faith communities cannot have the penny and the bun.

Extreme action for God

Cohesion is most seriously threatened when believers think they are justified in taking any action, even the most extreme, to defend or propagate the faith – the third threat noted above. The question that has to be faced by believers is whether such an attitude is actually the logical end-point of all religious believing. This is certainly what many of the more vocal critics of religious faith believe. They would argue that believers think they have a monopoly of religious truth: that God has entrusted this truth to them and they must, therefore, defend it or further its progress, even to the point of laying down their lives or other people's; that there is no reason to learn from others, including people of another faith, since others have nothing of importance to impart and can only confuse or lead astray. Accordingly, they attempt to ensure that everyone believes what they believe. This is why the history of religion, so the argument goes, is a history of coercion and violence in the name of God. For the religious impulse is always towards uniformity – hence the Holy Inquisition, hence *fatwas*, hence the burning of *The Satanic Verses*, hence the shooting of doctors for performing abortions, hence the attacks on the London transport system. The only reason religions no longer behave like this in Western societies is because they have been subordinated to the secular state; but given a chance they will again seek to assert themselves.

If the logic of religion really does lead inescapably in this direction, then inevitably the world faces not just a global 'clash of civilizations', as the (Judaeo-Christian/secular) West squares up to a resurgent Islam, but also more localized conflicts between religious people and those who do not share their particular beliefs.[19] In other words, if religion abhors pluralism, in a plural society and a plural world, religion is a permanent threat to social and community cohesion.

The temptation of mild-mannered, liberal-minded believers of any religion in the British context is to dismiss such arguments out of hand. It seems absurd to suggest that they or their local congregation could ever resort to violence in the name of faith – and no doubt that is true. But such parochialism brings complacency. We have now seen in the UK, as well as elsewhere, extreme action in the name of religion. The question for our time, therefore, at the local, national and international level, is whether religion does commit believers to this pressure towards uniformity which under certain conditions can lead some believers to take extreme action, or whether religion can contribute towards making the plural world we live in, whose pluralism is mirrored in every urban community in Britain, 'safe for disagreement', including, and perhaps especially, religious disagreement.[20]

Making the world safe for disagreement

We accept too easily the idea that there are only two ways in which we can make sense of a plurality of religions in the world. The first is to assume that only one religion can be true – true in the sense of being universally true for all people and all times – and all the others must be false. The second is to assume that none is true because religion is not a matter of truth and falsity, but something else – a matter of personal taste, a universal delusion, an expression of an emotional or ethical commitment. Contemporary atheistic dismissals of religion can attack from either of these two directions, seeing it as arrogantly absolutist or merely subjective, though in recent years attacks have tended to assume that religion commits its adherents to believe that they and they alone hold God-given truths and everyone else is mired in varying degrees of satanic darkness and delusion.

But both of these accounts – the absolute and the relative – must be resisted; for relativism leads to the trivialization of other people's beliefs, and so indifference towards them; while absolutism leads to their dismissal, which could threaten cohesion. I say 'could' threaten cohesion because it does not necessarily follow that the person who believes their faith is the only route to salvation for all would necessarily think it was right to impose it on others by any means. One could be a liberal and an absolutist and, of course, the liberal state would not permit illiberal proselytizing, pressurizing or indoctrinating.

Nevertheless, I want to ask whether a plural society such as ours is not potentially threatened by each of these approaches. At one time the relativism of multiculturalism seemed like a way forward, but religious people have come to reject it because of the way it breeds indifference towards faith. Yet the alternative – accepting the truth of one religion and, by implication, dismissing the rest – makes us uncomfortable in a plural society. But if we turn from relativism, is that not where we end up – asserting our faith and dismissing everyone else's? The urgent question for these days, therefore, is whether this either/or – if not relativism then absolutism – is the only way forward; for if it is, and religious people take up an absolutist position, then some version of the clash of civilizations, however low-level, seems to be ever present, just below the surface.

I want to argue for pluralism, not in the sense that we live in a world of many faiths – that is obviously true – but in the sense that a plurality of faiths is both inevitable and healthy for the human race. It is, if you like, one of God's good gifts. What pluralism does is to open up the possibility of living life in a number of different ways and according to a range of different values, because an inescapably plural world is a world that does not narrow or close down possibilities for how individuals may live. Pluralism protects from a stultifying uniformity.

Following Isaiah Berlin, let us call the belief that one's own religion is uniquely true 'monism' (and this can embrace non-religious world-views as well). Monists believe there can only be one truth, one correct answer to questions about faith and values, about God and the world, and it is theirs. Here we might recall how Stuart Hampshire summed it up above: 'Obviously, if one God, only one morality – His law and the falsity of moral pluralism therefore.'[21] Monists are not necessarily aggressive and antagonistic towards those who do not agree with them. They can be tolerant of other points of view; but it is a particular kind of tolerance – the tolerance that bides its time, a patronizing tolerance that believes that sooner or later the falsity of other positions will become clear. (Any Protestant who has taken part in doctrinal conversations with Roman Catholics will know exactly what I mean – you always know that the Roman Catholic conversationalist never really accepts that this can be an acceptable route to religious truth.) Of course, tolerance of this kind is better for social cohesion than antagonism. But is it the only way forward? If it is, it is rather fragile, likely to break down at any moment, especially if a person feels the future of their religion (the truth the world needs) is at stake.

Isaiah Berlin traces monism back to its origins in Platonic thought. It is a belief

> in the first place that, as in the sciences, all genuine questions must have one true answer and one only, all the rest being necessarily errors; in the second place, that there must be a dependable path towards the discovery of these truths; in the third place, that the true answers, when found, must necessarily be compatible with one another and form a single whole, for one truth cannot be incompatible with another – that we knew a priori . . . In the case of morals, we could then conceive what the perfect life must be, founded as it would be on a correct under- standing of the rules that governed the universe.[22]

We may not achieve this perfect knowledge but we know that

> the answers must be known to someone: perhaps Adam in Paradise knew; perhaps we shall only reach them at the end of days; if men cannot know them, perhaps the angels know; and if not the angels, then God knows. These timeless truths must in principle be knowable.[23]

Monism entered Christian thinking by way of the Greeks and has a long history. But the absolutist position was at its most intense in the Roman Catholic Church during the nineteenth century, in reaction to growing secularization and the advance of modernity. In 1864, the Church produced a Syllabus of Errors that itemized and con- demned every feature of the modern world – including democracy, progress and liberalism. The assertion of absolutism reached its peak in 1870 with the Declaration of Papal Infallibility: when the Pope made an *ex cathedra* pronouncement in matters of faith and morals this was held to be infallible. It is probably this baleful period of Catholic history that colours the mind of many contemporary crit- ics of Christianity. But critics can also be seduced by the scientific paradigm where there can only be a single truth. Richard Dawkins, in his consideration of religion, assumes that people of faith must likewise believe in the unique truth of their own religion and regard everyone else as either muddle-headed or satanically mistaken. But does religion inevitably commit the believer to such a monist position? In other words, how do people of faith deal with the matter of religious pluralism?

We ought to note in the first place that within the monotheistic faiths there is the idea of God's revelation being to some people and not necessarily to all – at least there is in Judaism and Islam. According to the Hebrew Bible, God's call is to the Jewish people; the laws of the Torah are binding on Jews in particular not all people in general. After Babel the human community is fragmented with many languages and cultures, each people having their own route to salvation. This is why, as Jonathan Sacks has pointed out, Judaism has no equivalent of the Christian doctrine of *extra ecclesiam non est salus* (there is no salvation outside the church).[24] Other people will have their own relationship with God. Similarly in the Qur'an there is this passage that speaks of God appointing different laws for different people:

> To each among you have We prescribed a Law and an Open Way. If Allah had so willed, He would have made you a single people, but (His plan is) to test you in what He hath given you: so strive as in a race in all virtues. The goal of you all is to Allah; it is He that will show you the truth of the matters in which you dispute . . .   (Q5.48)

Christianity is theoretically less amenable to the idea of pluralism ('No one comes to the Father but by me'[25]), but when you examine the history of Christian belief and practice, what stands out is not so much the uniformity as the diversity. Church officials, from the grandest prelate to the humblest parish priest, have always wanted doctrinal and liturgical uniformity, and uniformity of values. But what we so often see is a remarkable degree of pluralism. Likewise, Judaism and Islam are both marked by differences, Orthodox and Reformed, Sunni and Shia. When we extend our vision to encompass all people and cultures, then the variety is even greater and more bewildering. Berlin notes this plurality of values that people seek, and that they not only differ, but in some respects they are incommensurable; we cannot simply adopt them all. Nevertheless, 'there is not an infinity of them: the number of human values, of values which I can pursue while maintaining my human semblance, my human character, is finite . . .'. Nor are we incapable of understanding why people pursue values that differ from our own:

... if a man pursues one of these values, I, who do not, am able to understand why he pursues it or what it would be like, in his circumstances, for me to be induced to pursue it. Hence the possibility of human understanding.[26]

This great diversity of values does not mean that we have to accept all of them as equally worthwhile. We form judgements based on our own particular circumstances, history and commitments, while recognizing that we do so from one particular perspective, shaped by our unique cultural history, and not from any position of privilege outside or above culture and history. But because values are sometimes incompatible, a society has to make up its mind at points of conflict which values are to prevail. This is not just a clash between competing religions or conflicting ideologies, but a clash within each set of values as well. So, for example, a country such as the UK, committed to a high degree of personal autonomy and freedom, may have to constrain that in the interest of national security.

Even so, we have to ask whether this plurality has been a weakness or a potential source of strength for the human community. If we think the latter, then we shall want to frame a theological understanding of God and his relationship to the world that allows for this variety. This is the great challenge to religious people in a plural society like ours. It involves recognizing at least three things.

Divine and human perspectives

The starting-point for any theological recognition of pluralism has to be being very clear that while God may stand outside history and culture, we do not. We have no God's-eye view of the world and its competing values, and therefore no way of deciding between ultimate values when they conflict. Believers look for security and think this is to be found in some unchanging and infallible tradition, including a holy scripture; but this is an illusion. Scripture needs interpreting and applying in particular situations – and we know that as soon as this happens there can be differences between us. This does not mean we are reduced to paralysis and can never embrace a particular faith and its values. We have no choice since we have to live out our lives according to some ultimate values. We try to ensure that they are consistent and coherent. But we can never view them from God's perspective. Perhaps this is why, as a matter of fact, on ethical and doctrinal issues, the popes have almost never made *ex cathedra* pronouncements on anything, even though in theory they could resolve everything!

All religious traditions adjust to changing circumstances. Acknowledging that is not easy for religions that ground their teaching on holy scriptures. We need ways of moving to new interpretations, ways of finding fresh insights in familiar texts. One way is to first read the text 'contextually', setting it in its *Sitz im Leben* (setting in life) before considering how it might apply in a contemporary situation. This task is at present more developed among Christians and Jews. There is a long history of interpreting the Bible in this way, using the tools of historical and literary criticism. In one respect, the nature of the Bible almost requires this since the different books were written over a long period of time, with different authors, and address very different situations. Congregations, as well as biblical scholars, are used to thinking about the circumstances that made this writer say what he said, before they turn to the question of the relevance of the text, if any, for today. In other words, believers have become more sophisticated in their use of scripture, learning not to draw a straight line from a scriptural passage to a present situation, but appreciating first the original context before seeing whether or how it might have a contemporary relevance.

But the Muslim scriptures are not of this kind. They are not arranged chronologically but by length of chapter, so that understanding the context is more difficult. They are not the work of many hands but come through one man, the Prophet Muhammad. Moreover, according to Muslim theology, no human agency is involved in their composition. Muhammad was merely the human conduit through whom the words of Allah came. This Qur'anic revelation exists eternally but is made available through the Prophet, producing in the believer an attitude of considerable awe towards the Qur'anic text. This was brought home to me many years ago when as a young priest I was asked by members of the Attercliffe mosque in Sheffield to come and meet the new imam. He was very young, immaculately dressed in white robes, and had only recently flown in from Pakistan. He spoke no English. I asked why they wanted an imam who could not speak English. They invited me to sit down with them, and all became clear. The young man began to recite the Qur'an. His voice was confident and very beautiful. He knew the (Arabic) Qur'an by heart. As he recited, I looked at the old men who sat round him in a half circle. Tears streamed from their eyes. This was a moment of supreme religious experience; for they were hearing the very speech of God. To hear the Qur'an is to hear God speak. It is but a short step from believing this is the speech of God to believing that what Allah is saying in one context is being spoken directly into the contemporary context.

The same applies to the Prophet himself. Although Muslims are clear that Muhammad is not divine, he is treated with a similar love, awe and respect to that Christians show towards Jesus Christ, who in Christian orthodoxy is divine. In his life – recorded in collections of his words and deeds (the hadith) – Muhammad is the living embodiment of the Qur'an. Pious Muslims seek, therefore, to model their lives now on his life then. But what does this mean? How far can lines be drawn from the life of someone in eighth-century Arabia to the life of a contemporary British Muslim? There is considerable theological work to be done by Islamic scholars who live in non-Muslim countries, and very little historical precedent to guide them.

But if Muslims do not learn how to read their scriptures and the hadith contextually, there will be conflicts between the faith and the modern world. We have seen this in relation to social institutions such as marriage, to ethical issues such as the treatment of homosexuals, and around the idea of *jihad*.

Irreconcilable differences

The second thing to note is that every religious tradition is internally pluralistic, with differences of interpretation that cannot be reconciled. This is less of a problem for Jews, who are used to lively and ongoing debate about the meaning of texts. 'Does not every text have 70 meanings?' Christians are less happy with it – the impulse in Christianity has invariably been to try to close debate, to resolve issues in creeds and confessions. But even Christians are aware that different interpretations are reflected in the New Testament itself. Despite the fact that the writers may want to take a monist or absolutist position, the collected books actually witness to pluralism. Even something as fundamental as who Jesus is receives a variety of treatments: from the spare, breathless and austere Gospel of Mark, in which Christ dies broken and baffled ('Why have you forsaken me?'), to the profound philosophical reflections of the fourth Evangelist, for whom the Son of Man has everything within his knowledge and control – 'It is accomplished'. These are very different portraits of Jesus that are not wholly reconcilable. It is hardly surprising, therefore, that Christians have disagreed and do disagree over how particular passages of scripture should be interpreted and what they mean for living the Christian life now. In Islam, although plurality can hardly be denied – Sunni, Shia, Sufi, together with different schools of jurisprudence – there is nevertheless a strong impulse against new interpretations. Muslims tend to value *taqlid* rather than *ijtihad*, preservation rather than innovation.

Possessing a holy scripture does not guarantee unity: it is not the end of division but its source. In which case, believers ought to be able to take a plural society in their stride.

Living with pluralism

So we find, in the third place, that different interpretations of the scriptures lead to different ways in which the religious life is to be lived out. For instance, there are some Christian communities who believe profoundly that following Christ commits disciples to repudiating any form of violence – the Amish, Quakers, Mennonites – while others puzzle over the meaning of a just war in a nuclear context. The liberal state required Christians to acquiesce in living with these denominational differences without recourse to violence or repression. Over time we found that what began as toleration eventually resulted in discovering much in each other's tradition that was valuable. We began to borrow from one another. The invitation to the world's religions now present in the UK is to embark on a similar ecumenical journey, from tolerance to discovery, made possible by mutual commitment to liberal values.

If religious people can learn to recognize the pluralism in their own traditions and the pluralism of the world, and to see both as a source of strength rather than weakness, then religion need not be a threat to social and community cohesion. But if religious people cannot do this, then in the inevitable struggles between groups, religion will again become a marker of identity and boundary; and on the wider stage a running battle of civilizations will be the dismal prospect awaiting us.

Summary and conclusion

This enquiry began with the question, 'Does religion help or hinder community cohesion?' Max Weber once said that 'the ultimately possible attitudes towards life are irreconcilable, and hence their struggle can never be brought to a final conclusion'.[27] The same point has been made even more forcibly by Isaiah Berlin. If we live in a plural society in which it is in the end impossible to reconcile religious (and other) beliefs – and we do – we must value those institutions and conventions that enable us to live together harmoniously. This is what Western societies have struggled over centuries to find and why the core values (contractual arrangements) of Western societies are so important for social and community cohesion. We cohere as a plural society around the key values of the democratic state. Once those values are repudiated, social and community cohesion is gravely threatened.

The cohesion of any dynamic society is necessarily precarious because in every society there is the potential for conflict as groups jostle for power, influence or scarce resources. Conflicts arise for many reasons, rarely for a single one. What we learn from various conflicts across the contemporary world is that in times of tension or conflict between groups, religion may play a negative or positive role. Negatively, religion can become a significant marker of difference, even if it is not the principal cause of the conflict or not a cause at all. Religion can mediate other differences that are significant – economic, social, political, ethnic. In the Balkans, Serbs reached for the symbols of their Orthodox Christianity even as Kosovan Albanians asserted their Islamic faith. The Burnley Project research suggested that in some white, working-class areas religion does not play a great part in people's day-to-day lives, but people may still understand themselves as 'Christian'. In times of tension this latent aspect of identity could be pressed into service as a way of marking the difference between the white and Asian communities – (white) Christians over against (Asian) Muslims. Symbols of Christianity – the cross, the flag of St George – may then be utilized as tokens of difference and signifiers of boundaries. Those on the extreme right of politics understand this very well and would exploit these symbols in the future as they have in the past. Similarly, for those in the minority cultures, if they feel that their community is threatened, religion may become one of the key markers of difference for them, however distanced they may personally have become from the mosque. Religion can play this role because these markers of difference related to culture, history and place are very deep within all of us. However fuzzy, we all have ideas about who we are, where we came from and where we belong. On the whole this is good; it brings people together and promotes solidarity and cohesion. It can equally well be used to distinguish 'us' from 'them'.

Religion is a powerful motivator, but this can cut two ways. It can lead men and women to see themselves as over against their neighbour, even to the point where their neighbour is their enemy. Yet if the tradition can be read differently, it can lead them to abhor violence and work for the good of their communities in the most selfless and sacrificial way. What will make the difference is whether believers can learn to embrace pluralism not as a threat to God's plan for the world but as an essential element in it.

This must now become the urgent agenda of the faith communities.

Appendix

Extract from A Shared Act of Commitment and Reflection by the Faith Communities of the United Kingdom

---

An Act of Commitment

Representatives from the faith communities and members of the audience join in an Act of Commitment to mark the year 2000.

Faith community representatives:

In a world scarred by the evils of war, racism, injustice and poverty, we offer this joint Act of Commitment as we look to our shared future.

All:

We commit ourselves
as people of many faiths,
to work together
for the common good,
uniting to build a better society,
grounded in values and ideals we share:

community,
personal integrity,
a sense of right and wrong,
learning, wisdom and love of truth,

care and compassion,
justice and peace,
respect for one another,
for the earth and its creatures.

We commit ourselves,
in a spirit of friendship and co-operation,

to work together
alongside all who share our values and ideals,
to help bring about a better world
now and for generations to come.

Source: <www.interfaith.org.uk/publications/brochure3100.htm>.

Notes

Introduction

1 John Gray, *Guardian*, 15 March 2008.
2 David Blunkett, in the Foreword to *Working Together: Co-operation Between Government and Faith Communities* (Faith Communities Unit, Home Office, 2004).
3 Before 1990, immigration was mainly from Commonwealth countries in South Asia and the Caribbean. Between 1992 and 2002, Britain had net inward migration from a much bigger spread of countries. The current figure for net migration following arrivals from Eastern Europe after 2004 is 223,000.
4 See Stephen Castles and Mark J. Miller, *The Age of Migration: International Population Movements in the Modern World* (Basingstoke: Macmillan, 1993).
5 Following the destruction by the Romans of the Temple in 70 CE at the close of the Jewish War, and after they put down Bar Kokhba's revolt in 132, Jews existed as minorities within other cultures until 1948, when modern Israel was created.
6 Unlike Christianity, which began as a minority faith in non-Christian cultures, Islam expanded by successful conquest across the Middle East and North Africa and into Western Europe, remaining dominant until the modern period.

1 Why 'community cohesion'?

1 George Orwell, *The Lion and the Unicorn: Socialism and the English Genius* (London: Secker & Warburg, 1941), p. 33.
2 In October 2007 the Chancellor of the Exchequer announced a new cross-government public service agreement (PSA 21) 'to build cohesive, empowered and active communities' – a commitment in 'The Government's Response to the Commission on Integration and Cohesion' (Department for Communities and Local Government, 2008), p. 7.
3 'Citizenship Survey' (Home Office), 2004.
4 The last line of the poem 'Jerusalem' by William Blake (1757–1827). 'Jerusalem' was a universally popular hymn, sung in church, at football matches by working-class men and before meetings of the Women's Institute by middle-class women.
5 Lorna Sage, *Bad Blood: A Memoir* (London: Fourth Estate, 2000), p. 4.

127

6 'If, then, faith is to be active in love, and if justice in the huge and imper-
sonal collectivities of contemporary life is love operating at a distance,
how are the energies of love to be related to that practical ordering of
life in community which is called politics?' Joseph Sittler, *The Structure
of Christian Ethics* (Louisville, KY: Westminster John Knox Press, 1998
[reissue of 1958 edn]), p. 79. A similar theme can be found in Reinhold
Niebuhr, *Moral Man and Immoral Society: A Study in Ethics and Politics*
(New York: Charles Scribner's Sons, 1932).

7 Much of my experience in the Midlands is echoed in Michael Young,
Family and Kinship in East London (London: Routledge & Kegan Paul,
1957).

8 My wife points out that it would have been more difficult for me had
I been a girl since the number of girls' grammar school places was
considerably lower than that for boys – the assumptions being that girls
were in general not as bright and most would prefer to leave and get
married. The things that made a difference for girls were: the raising of
the school-leaving age – previously many had left school before taking
public examinations and had no idea they could achieve results on a par
with boys; the high levels of unemployment in the 1970s, which resulted
in more girls staying longer in education; and the expansion of higher
education.

9 By 1957, the Prime Minister of the day, Harold Macmillan, felt able
to say that the country was enjoying 'a state of prosperity such as we
have never had in my life-time – nor indeed ever in the history of this
country'. Cited in Anthony Sampson, *Macmillan: A Study in Ambiguity*
(London: Penguin, 1967), p. 159.

10 Clause Four reads in full: 'To secure for the workers by hand or by brain
the full fruits of their industry and the most equitable distribution
thereof that may be possible upon the basis of the common ownership
of the means of production, distribution and exchange, and the best
obtainable system of popular administration and control of each industry or service.' It was adopted by the Party in 1918 and substantially
amended in 1995.

11 Stephen Spender's poem, 'My parents kept me from children who were
rough', exactly summed up this aspect of my childhood.

12 Richard Layard, 'Towards a happier society' (*New Statesman*, 24 February
2003).

13 The amended clause reads: 'The Labour Party is a democratic socialist
party. It believes that by the strength of our common endeavour we
achieve more than we achieve alone, so as to create for each of us the
means to realise our true potential and for all of us a community in
which power, wealth and opportunity are in the hands of the many, not
the few, where the rights we enjoy reflect the duties we owe, and where
we live together, freely, in a spirit of solidarity, tolerance and respect.'

14 Keith Robbins, *History, Religion and Identity in Modern Britain* (London: Hambledon, 1993), p. 195.

15 Hugh McLeod, *The Religious Crisis of the 1960s* (Oxford: OUP, 2007).

16 Robert Shepherd, 'The real tributaries of Enoch's "rivers of blood"', *Spectator*, 1 March 2008. Powell had opposed Indian independence on the grounds that communalism would make the country ungovernable.

17 The riots were over several days in Watts, a suburb of Los Angeles, inhabited by African Americans.

18 Marjorie Jones was the wife of the editor of the *Express and Star* newspaper.

19 Arthur Marwick, *British Society since 1945* (London: Penguin, 1990), p. 165.

20 This point has been made by Trevor Phillips, Chair of the Commission for Equality and Human Rights. Predictably, if disappointingly, he has been accused by some of racism.

21 'The Brixton Disorders 10–12 April 1981: Report of an Inquiry by Lord Scarman' (London: HMSO, 1981).

22 Leslie Page Moch, *Moving Europeans: Migrations in Western Europe since 1650*, 2nd edn (Bloomington, IN: University of Indiana Press, 2003), p. 189.

23 Edward Heath – Margaret Thatcher's predecessor as Conservative leader – was deeply marked by his experience of the pre-war depression and believed that political solutions had to be firmly based in a coherent set of moral principles. See his Foreword to William Temple, *Christianity and Social Order* (London: Shepheard-Walwyn/SPCK, 1976).

24 Norman Tebbit was speaking at the Conservative Party Conference as Secretary of State for Employment following the Brixton and Handsworth riots.

25 A former Conservative Prime Minister, Harold Macmillan, was appalled by this and in his maiden speech in the House of Lords asked rhetorically whether the fathers of the Durham miners had not fought in two world wars. See Noël Annan, *Our Age: The Generation that Made Post-War Britain* (London: Fontana, 1991), p. 574.

26 Church of England, Commission on Urban Priority Areas: *Faith in the City: A Call for Action by Church and Nation* (London: Church House Publishing, 1985).

27 Q22.52. See also Q53.23.

28 A good explanation of the verses and their history can be found in Martin Forward, *Muhammad: A Short Biography* (Oxford: Oneworld, 1997), pp. 34–6.

29 'Community Cohesion: A Report of the Independent Review Team', chaired by Ted Cantle (Home Office, 2001).

30 Ted Cantle, *Community Cohesion: A New Framework for Race and Diversity* (Basingstoke: Palgrave Macmillan, 2005), p. 48.
31 Ferdinand Tönnies (ed./tr. Charles P. Loomis), *Community and Society* (New York: Harper & Row, 1963), p. 47.
32 Quoted in Zygmunt Bauman, *Community: Seeking Safety in an Insecure World* (Cambridge: Polity, 2000), p. 10.
33 Alexis de Tocqueville, *Democracy in America and Two Essays on America* (London: Penguin, 2003).
34 de Tocqueville, *Democracy*, p. 513.
35 For a full discussion of the term 'community cohesion', see: 'Community Cohesion: A Literature Review', Centre for Research in Ethnic Relations, University of Warwick, Coventry, CV4 7AL.
36 'Guidance on Community Cohesion' (Local Government Association, 2002).
37 'Our Shared Future' (Department for Communities and Local Government, 2007).
38 'The Government's Response to the Commission on Integration and Cohesion', p. 10.
39 The London bombings were on 7 July 2005. They killed 52 commuters and injured 700.
40 al-Jazeera, 1 September 2005.
41 Four men were eventually tried and convicted.
42 Two men were identified at Glasgow: Bilal Abdullah was a British-born doctor of Iraqi descent; the driver was thought to be Kafeel Ahmed, who died of his burns. They left a suicide note. Eight people were arrested following incidents in London outside a nightclub.
43 The lecture, 'Civil and Religious Law in England: A religious perspective', was the first of a series on Islam and English Law sponsored by the University of London and the Temple Church.

2 The contribution of faith to community cohesion

1 See Alan Billings, *Dying and Grieving: A Guide to Pastoral Ministry* (London: SPCK, 2002).
2 Lyda Judson Hanifan, 'The Rural School Community Centre' (*Annals of the American Academy of Political and Social Science*, 67, 1916), cited in Robert D. Putnam, *Bowling Alone: The Collapse and Revival of American Community* (New York: Simon & Schuster, 2000), p. 19.
3 See Andrew Holden, *Jehovah's Witnesses: Portrait of a Contemporary Religious Movement* (London: Routledge, 2002).
4 Alison Gilchrist, *The Well-Connected Community: A Networking Approach to Community Development* (Bristol: Policy Press, 2004). See also '"Face-to-Face and Side-by-Side": A framework for inter faith dialogue and social action' (Department for Communities and Local Government, 2008).

5 Hugh McLeod, *The Religious Crisis of the 1960s* (Oxford: OUP, 2007), p. 102.
6 This is charted in Michael Collins, *The Likes of Us: A Biography of the White Working Class* (London: Granta, 2004).
7 Alexis de Tocqueville, *Democracy in America and Two Essays on America* (London: Penguin, 2003).
8 *Sunday Telegraph*, 1 April 2007.
9 Putnam, *Bowling Alone*, pp. 283–4.
10 See Peter Brierley, *'Christian' England: What the 1989 English Church Census Reveals* (London: MARC Europe, 1991); Grace Davie, *Religion in Britain since 1945: Believing without Belonging* (Oxford: Blackwell, 1994), ch. 3.
11 Steve Bruce, *God is Dead: Secularization in the West* (Oxford: Blackwell, 2002) and *Religion in Modern Britain* (Oxford: OUP, 1995).
12 Callum Brown, *The Death of Christian Britain: Understanding Secularisation 1800–2000* (London: Routledge, 2000).
13 Brown, *Death of Christian Britain*, p. 198.
14 For converts to Islam, see Kate Zebiri, *British Muslim Converts: Choosing Alternative Lives* (London: Oneworld, 2008).
15 For a discussion of the issues, see Andrew Wright, *Critical Religious Education, Multiculturalism and the Pursuit of Truth* (Cardiff: University of Wales Press, 2007).
16 Matthew Guest, Karen Tusting and Linda Woodhead (eds), *Congregational Studies in the UK: Christianity in a Post-Christian Context* (Aldershot: Ashgate, 2004); Paul Heelas and Linda Woodhead, *The Spiritual Revolution: Why Religion is Giving Way to Spirituality* (Oxford: Blackwell, 2004).
17 The same phenomenon is found in the USA, as Putnam notes – see Putnam, *Bowling Alone*, ch. 4.
18 Evangelicalism is not a denomination. Evangelical churches may be free of any wider institutional allegiance or may be part of an older mainstream tradition. If they are the latter, they may choose to play little part in the affairs of the parent body, preferring the company of other evangelicals of any denomination or none.
19 Linda Woodhead and Paul Heelas (eds), *Religion in Modern Times: An Interpretive Anthology* (Oxford: Blackwell, 2000).
20 See my *Secular Lives Sacred Hearts: The Role of the Church in a Time of No Religion* (London: SPCK, 2005).
21 Billings, *Secular Lives* and *Dying and Grieving*.
22 Grace Davie, *Religion in Britain since 1945*; *Religion in Modern Europe: A Memory Mutates* (Oxford: OUP, 2000); *The Sociology of Religion* (London: Sage, 2007).
23 McLeod, *Religious Crisis*, p. 1.
24 *Guardian*, 15 March 2008.

25 Tom Butler, in his Foreword to Julie Lewis, with Elizabeth Randolph-Horn, *Faiths, Hope and Participation: Celebrating Faith Groups' Role in Neighbourhood Renewal* (London: New Economics Foundation and Church Urban Fund, 2001).

26 Foreword to 'Working Together: Co-operation between Government and Faith Communities' (Home Office, 2004).

27 William Wilberforce, who opposed slavery and the slave trade; Elizabeth Fry, the prison reformer; and Lord Shaftesbury, who introduced legislation regulating factory conditions, were all religiously inspired.

28 Cited in ' "Face-to-Face and Side-by-Side": A framework for inter faith dialogue and social action' (Department for Communities and Local Government, 2007), p. 25.

29 This is in addition to the Church's fund-raising for overseas work – Christian Aid (Anglican and Free Churches), Tearfund (Evangelical) and Cafod (Roman Catholic).

30 Church Urban Fund website, <www.cuf.org.uk>.

31 The government has noted that research shows that people taking part in cultural activities were 20 per cent more likely to know 'many people' in their neighbourhood, and 60 per cent more likely to believe that 'many of their neighbours can be trusted'. 'Taking Part Survey' (Department for Culture, Media and Sport, 2006).

32 'Citizenship Survey' (Home Office/Department for Communities and Local Government, 2005).

33 Putnam, *Bowling Alone*, p. 66.

34 Putnam, *Bowling Alone*, p. 65.

35 The 1851 census was unusual in that it had appended to it religious questions asking for information on church attendances. These were not compulsory. For details, see Owen Chadwick, *The Victorian Church. Part One, 1829–1859* (London, SCM, 1987), pp. 363ff.

36 For information on converts, see Zebiri, *British Muslim Converts*.

37 Mrs C. F. Alexander famously turned the teaching of the Catechism into a very popular hymn, 'All things bright and beautiful', including a verse reflecting this answer:

> The rich man in his castle,
> The poor man at his gate;
> God made them, high or lowly,
> And ordered their estate.

38 Rumman Ahmed, in his Foreword to Lewis, *Faiths, Hope and Participation*.

39 Groups such as the Jehovah's Witnesses will build up bonding social capital but not bridging. They do not encourage their members to be active citizens but to concentrate on spreading their exclusive message. See Holden, *Jehovah's Witnesses*. Research indicates that

participation and volunteering is lower among young Muslims than members of other faith groups. 'Citizenship Survey' (Home Office, 2001).

40 Lewis, *Faiths, Hope and Participation*, 5:31.

41 'Involving Communities in Urban and Rural Regeneration: a Guide for Practitioners' (Department for Environment, Transport and the Regions, 1997).

42 Christie Davies, 'Crime and the rise and decline of the relational society', in Jonathan Burnside and Nicola Baker (eds), *Relational Justice: Repairing the Breach* (Winchester: Waterside, 1994), pp. 31–41.

43 The figures are from Professor Davies.

44 Historically evangelicals have a long record of engagement with wider society and social concerns. The Evangelical Alliance – an umbrella organization – seeks to revive and continue that tradition.

45 The more recent Anglican rites of baptism and confirmation encourage this within the service.

46 Heelas and Woodhead, *Spiritual Revolution*.

47 See Charles Taylor, *A Secular Age* (London: Belknap, 2007), ch. 13.

48 Akbar S. Ahmed, *Discovering Islam: Making Sense of Muslim History and Society* (London: Routledge, 1988).

49 Ed Husain, *The Islamist: Why I Joined Radical Islam in Britain, What I Saw Inside and Why I Left* (London: Penguin, 2007); Charles Allen, *God's Terrorists: The Wahabbi Cult and the Hidden Roots of Modern Jihad* (London: Little, Brown, 2006); Gilles Kepel, *Jihad: The Trail of Political Islam* (London: Tauris, 2002).

50 Philip Lewis, *Islamic Britain: Religion, Politics and Identity among British Muslims* (London: Tauris, 1994), p. 16.

51 Fred Halliday, *Arabs in Exile: Yemeni Migrants in Urban Britain* (London: Tauris, 1992), quoted in Lewis, *Islamic Britain*, p. 17.

52 Putnam, *Bowling Alone*, p. 67.

3 Do 'parallel lives' threaten community cohesion?

1 'Community Cohesion: A Report of the Independent Review Team', chaired by Ted Cantle (Home Office, 2001).

2 See also Munira Mirza, Abi Senthilkumaran and Zein Ja'far, *Living Apart Together: British Muslims and the Paradox of Multi-Culturalism* (London: Policy Exchange, 2007).

3 Alan Billings and Andrew Holden, 'Interfaith Interventions and Cohesive Communities: The effectiveness of interfaith activity in towns marked by enclavisation and parallel lives' (Lancaster University, 2007).

4 See Leslie Page Moch, *Moving Europeans: Migrations in Western Europe since 1650*, 2nd edn (Bloomington, IN: University of Indiana Press, 2003), ch. 5.

5 Ted Cantle, 'The End of Parallel Lives? Final Report of the Community Cohesion Panel' (Home Office, 2004).

6 From a private conversation. The estate agent told me of a movement of prosperous Sikh families to towns such as Market Harborough.

7 Billings and Holden, 'Interfaith Interventions', Appendix E.

8 Robert D. Putnam, *Bowling Alone: The Collapse and Revival of American Community* (New York: Simon & Schuster, 2000), p. 371.

9 Association of Metropolitan Authorities, 'Housing and Race: Policy and Practice in Local Authorities' (AMA, 1985).

10 This section is drawn from Billings and Holden, 'Interfaith Interventions'.

11 <www.lancs.ac.uk/fass/religstudies/research/projects/burnley.htm>.

12 Research by Saffron Karlsen and James Nazroo of the Understanding Population and Trends Programme, cited in *Britain Today* (ESRC, 2007), pp. 54–5. Also confirmed by the Home Office 'Citizenship Survey', 2003. This found that while all ethnic groups felt that they 'belonged' in Britain (whites 86.7 per cent; Muslims 85.97 per cent), those least at home were Caribbeans (79 per cent) and Africans (74.5 per cent).

13 See S. Rizvi, 'New Cultures, Security and Transnational Belonging: Cross-generational Perspectives among British Pakistani Women', *European Journal of Cultural Studies*, Vol. 10, No. 3, 2007, pp. 327–42.

14 Jonathan Sacks, *Faith in the Future* (London: Darton, Longman & Todd, 1995), pp. 78–9.

15 Cited by Hazel Blears in the Foreword to ' "Face-to-Face and Side-by-Side": A framework for inter-faith dialogue and social action' (Department for Communities and Local Government, 2008), p. 6.

16 There are some 45 branches throughout the country.

17 *Inter Faith Organisations in the UK: A Directory*, 4th edn (London: Inter Faith Network for the United Kingdom, 2007).

18 Points made in Robert Furbey, Adam Dinham, Richard Farnell, Doreen Finneron and Guy Wilkinson, *Faith as Social Capital: Connecting or Dividing* (Bristol: Policy Press/Joseph Rowntree Foundation, 2006).

19 See Shiv Malik, 'My brother the bomber', *Prospect*, June 2007, p. 34.

20 Malik, 'My brother'.

21 ' "Face-to-Face and Side-by-Side", p. 13.

22 Some 65 per cent of people thought there should be more mixing across ethnic divisions. 'Citizenship Survey' (Department for Communities and Local Government, 2007).

23 The School Linking Network was launched in 2007 to bring together schools of different faiths, social settings and ethnicities. Local authorities can also support these types of initiatives through their Standing Advisory Council on Religious Education (SACRE) – a local interfaith body.

4 Does religion threaten community cohesion?

1 'So potent was religion in persuading to evil deeds.' Titus Lucretius Carus, *De Rerum Natura*, Book I, 101.
2 This was one of the findings of a public consultation by the Joseph Rowntree Foundation in 2008, 'What are today's social evils?' See .
3 Richard Dawkins, *The God Delusion* (London: Bantam, 2006) and Christopher Hitchens, *God is not Great: The Case Against Religion* (London: Atlantic Books, 2007) strongly make this point.
4 For a balanced discussion and a criticism of part of the Dawkins thesis, see David Martin, *Does Christianity Cause War?* (Oxford: OUP, 1997).
5 Quoted in Steve Bruce, *Paisley: Religion and Politics in Northern Ireland* (Oxford: OUP, 2007), p. 249.
6 'Thought for the Day', BBC Radio 4, 25 March 2008.
7 Interviewed in *The Times* by Mark Henderson, 29 March 2008.
8 *Church Times*, 28 March 2008.
9 Paul Vallely, 'This does not violate a deep taboo', *Church Times*, 28 March 2008.
10 One historian, William Thomas Whitley, wrote: 'Politically it is a constant experience that Catholics and Moslems are never content with mere equality, but on principle, always aim at superiority. And their widespread geographic adherents give them political means which they are seldom averse to use, to the detriment of both civil and religious liberty.' Cited in L. E. Elliott-Binns, *Religion in the Victorian Era* (London: Lutterworth, 1964), pp. 126–7.
11 The lecture, 'Civil and Religious Law in England: A religious perspective', was the first of a series on Islam and English Law sponsored by the University of London and the Temple Church.
12 This point was well made by David Rankin and Lee A. Casey in 'Toleration and Islamic Law', *The Wall Street Journal*, 12 February 2008.
13 *The Times*, 12 February 2008.
14 *Independent*, 13 February 2008.
15 *Daily Telegraph*, 12 February 2008.
16 *The Times*, 9 February 2008. See also Stephen Schwartz, who makes similar points in 'Sharia Comes for the Archbishop', *Weekly Standard*, 25 February 2008.
17 *The Times*, 12 March 2008.
18 David Waines, *An Introduction to Islam* (Cambridge: CUP, 1995), p. 212.
19 Ernest Gellner, Foreword to Akbar Ahmed and Hastings Donnan, *Islam, Globalization and Postmodernity* (London: Routledge, 1994), p. xi.
20 Waines, *An Introduction*, p. 212.
21 Sayyid Qutb, *Milestones* (Delhi: Markazi Maktaba Islami, 1981).

22 Ed Husain, *The Islamist: Why I Joined Radical Islam in Britain, What I Saw Inside and Why I Left* (London: Penguin, 2007); Shiv Malik, 'My brother the bomber', *Prospect*, June 2007.

23 Malik, 'My brother', p. 36.

24 Malik, 'My brother', p. 36.

25 Hassan Butt, quoted in Malik, 'My brother', p. 37.

26 Malik, 'My brother', p. 41.

27 Hassan Butt, *The Times*, 14 July 2007.

28 Malik, 'My brother', p. 33.

5 Faith's ambiguous presence

1 Giancarlo Collet noted this plea for a greater understanding of immigrants scribbled across an advertisement. Giancarlo Collet, 'From Theological Vandalism to Theological Romanticism? Questions about a Multicultural Identity of Christianity', in Norbert Greinacher and Norbert Mette (eds), *Christianity and Cultures: A Mutual Enrichment* (London: SCM, 1994), p. 25.

2 David Blunkett's speech to the Institute of Public Policy Research, 7 July 2004, 'New challenges for race equality and community cohesion in the twenty-first century' (Home Office, 2004), p. 7.

3 Stuart Hampshire, *Justice is Conflict* (Princeton, NJ: Princeton University Press, 2000), p. 47.

4 'Citizenship Survey', formerly undertaken by the Home Office but now the responsibility of the Department for Communities and Local Government.

5 ' "Face-to-Face and Side-by-Side": A framework for inter faith dialogue and social action' (Department for Communities and Local Government, 2007), p. 13.

6 BBC Ipsos/MORI Poll, April 2008.

7 Multiculturalism is criticized in Zygmunt Bauman, *Community: Seeking Safety in an Insecure World* (Cambridge: Polity, 2000). Later critics include the Ugandan-born journalist Yasmin Alibhai-Brown and Trevor Phillips, Chair of the Commission for Racial Equality.

8 Roy Jenkins' speech to the Voluntary Liaison Committees, London, 23 May 1966, cited in Ted Cantle, *Community Cohesion: A New Framework for Race and Diversity* (Basingstoke: Palgrave Macmillan, 2005), p. 83.

9 Bauman, *Community*, p. 136.

10 Frank Furedi, *Politics of Fear: Beyond Left and Right* (London: Continuum, 2005), p. 106.

11 Anthony Seldon, *Major: A Political Life* (London: Weidenfeld & Nicolson, 1997), p. 370.

12 Gordon Brown, in a speech to the Fabian Society in January 2006.

13 Isaiah Berlin, *Personal Impressions* (London: Pimlico, 1998), p. 257, cited in George Crowder and Henry Hardy, *The One and the Many: Reading Isaiah Berlin* (Amherst, NY: Prometheus, 2007), p. 20.
14 The term 'sacred canopy' is from Peter Berger, *The Social Reality of Religion* (Harmondsworth: Penguin, 1973).
15 Anthony Russell, *The Clerical Profession* (London: SPCK, 1984).
16 Russell, *Clerical Profession*, p. 148.
17 I have written about this in *Secular Lives Sacred Hearts: The Role of the Church in a Time of No Religion* (London: SPCK, 2005).
18 *BBC News*, 20 December 2004.
19 Samuel Huntington, *The Clash of Civilizations and the Remaking of World Order* (New York: Simon & Schuster, 1996).
20 Nicholas Rescher, *Pluralism: Against the Demand for Consensus* (Oxford: Clarendon, 1993), p. 5.
21 Hampshire, *Justice is Conflict*, p. 47.
22 Isaiah Berlin, *The Crooked Timber of Humanity: Chapters in the History of Human Ideas* (London: Fontana, 1991), pp. 5–6.
23 Berlin, *Crooked Timber*, p. 6.
24 Jonathan Sacks, *The Dignity of Difference: How to Avoid the Clash of Civilizations* (London: Continuum, 2003), p. 53.
25 John 14.6.
26 Isaiah Berlin, *The Power of Ideas* (London: Chatto & Windus, 2000), p. 12.
27 Cited in Crowder and Hardy, *The One and the Many*, p. 279.

Select bibliography

Ahmed, Akbar, *Discovering Islam: Making Sense of Muslim History and Society* (London: Routledge, 1988).

Ahmed, Akbar and Donnan, Hastings (eds), *Islam, Globalization and Postmodernity* (London: Routledge, 1994).

Allen, Charles, *God's Terrorists: The Wahabbi Cult and the Hidden Roots of Modern Jihad* (London: Little, Brown, 2006).

Annan, Noël, *Our Age: The Generation that Made Post-War Britain* (London: Fontana, 1991).

Bauman, Zygmunt, *Community: Seeking Safety in an Insecure World* (Cambridge: Polity, 2000).

Berger, Peter, *The Social Reality of Religion* (Harmondsworth: Penguin, 1973).

Berlin, Isaiah, *The Crooked Timber of Humanity: Chapters in the History of Human Ideas* (London: Fontana, 1991).

Berlin, Isaiah, *Personal Impressions* (London: Pimlico, 1998).

Berlin, Isaiah, *The Power of Ideas* (London: Chatto & Windus, 2000).

Billings, Alan, *Dying and Grieving: A Guide to Pastoral Ministry* (London: SPCK, 2002).

Billings, Alan, *Secular Lives Sacred Hearts: The Role of the Church in a Time of No Religion* (London: SPCK, 2005).

Brierley, Peter, *'Christian' England: What the 1989 English Church Census Reveals* (London: MARC Europe, 1991).

Brown, Callum, *The Death of Christian Britain: Understanding Secularisation 1800–2000* (London: Routledge, 2000).

Bruce, Steve, *Religion in Modern Britain* (Oxford: OUP, 1995).

Bruce, Steve, *God is Dead: Secularization in the West* (Oxford: Blackwell, 2002).

Bruce, Steve, *Paisley: Religion and Politics in Northern Ireland* (Oxford: OUP, 2007).

Burnside, Jonathan and Baker, Nicola (eds), *Relational Justice: Repairing the Breach* (Winchester: Waterside, 1994).

Cantle, Ted, *Community Cohesion: A New Framework for Race and Diversity* (Basingstoke: Palgrave Macmillan, 2005).

Castles, Stephen and Miller, Mark J., *The Age of Migration: International Population Movements in the Modern World* (Basingstoke: Macmillan, 1993).

Church of England, Commission on Urban Priority Areas: *Faith in the City: A Call for Action by Church and Nation* (London: Church House Publishing, 1985).

Collins, Michael, *The Likes of Us: A Biography of the White Working Class* (London: Granta, 2004).

Crowder, George and Hardy, Henry (eds), *The One and the Many: Reading Isaiah Berlin* (Amherst, NY: Prometheus, 2007).

Davie, Grace, *Religion in Britain since 1945: Believing without Belonging* (Oxford: Blackwell, 1994).

Davie, Grace, *Religion in Modern Europe: A Memory Mutates* (Oxford: OUP, 2000).

Davie, Grace, *The Sociology of Religion* (London: Sage, 2007).

De Tocqueville, Alexis, *Democracy in America and Two Essays on America* (London: Penguin, 2003).

Elliott-Binns, L. E., *Religion in the Victorian Era* (London: Lutterworth, 1964).

Forward, Martin, *Muhammad: A Short Biography* (Oxford: Oneworld, 1997).

Furedi, Frank, *Politics of Fear: Beyond Left and Right* (London: Continuum, 2005).

Gilchrist, Alison, *The Well-connected Community: A Networking Approach to Community Development* (Bristol: Policy Press, 2004).

Greinacher, Norbert and Mette, Norbert (eds), *Christianity and Cultures: A Mutual Enrichment* (London: SCM, 1994).

Guest, Matthew, Tusting, Karen and Woodhead, Linda (eds), *Congregational Studies in the UK: Christianity in a Post-Christian Context* (Aldershot: Ashgate, 2004).

Halliday, Fred, *Arabs in Exile: Yemeni Migrants in Urban Britain* (London: Tauris, 1992).

Hampshire, Stuart, *Justice is Conflict* (Princeton, NJ: Princeton University Press, 2000).

Heelas, Paul and Woodhead, Linda, *The Spiritual Revolution: Why Religion is Giving Way to Spirituality* (Oxford: Blackwell, 2004).

Holden, Andrew, *Jehovah's Witnesses: Portrait of a Contemporary Religious Movement* (London: Routledge, 2002).

Huntington, Samuel P., *The Clash of Civilizations and the Remaking of World Order* (New York: Simon & Schuster, 1996).

Husain, Ed, *The Islamist: Why I Joined Radical Islam in Britain, What I Saw Inside and Why I Left* (London: Penguin, 2007).

Kepel, Gilles, *Jihad: The Trail of Political Islam* (London: Tauris, 2002).

Lewis, Julie with Randolph-Horn, Elizabeth, *Faiths, Hope and Participation: Celebrating Faith Groups' Role in Neighbourhood Renewal* (London: New Economics Foundation and Church Urban Fund, 2001).

Lewis, Philip, *Islamic Britain: Religion, Politics and Identity among British Muslims* (London: Tauris, 1994).

Lucretius Carus, Titus (ed. C. Bailey), *De Rerum Natura* (Oxford: Clarendon, 1947).

McLeod, Hugh, *The Religious Crisis of the 1960s* (Oxford: OUP, 2007).

Martin, David, *Does Christianity Cause War?* (Oxford: OUP, 1997).

Marwick, Arthur, *British Society since 1945* (London: Penguin, 1990).

Moch, Leslie Page, *Moving Europeans: Migrations in Western Europe since 1650*, 2nd edn (Bloomington, IN: University of Indiana Press, 2003).

Orwell, George, *The Lion and the Unicorn: Socialism and the English Genius* (London: Secker & Warburg, 1941).

Putnam, Robert D., *Bowling Alone: The Collapse and Revival of American Community* (New York: Simon & Schuster, 2000).

Rescher, Nicholas, *Pluralism: Against the Demand for Consensus* (Oxford: Clarendon, 1993).

Robbins, Keith, *History, Religion and Identity in Modern Britain* (London: Hambledon, 1993).

Russell, Anthony, *The Clerical Profession* (London: SPCK, 1984).

Sacks, Jonathan, *Faith in the Future* (London: Darton, Longman & Todd, 1995).

Sacks, Jonathan, *The Dignity of Difference: How to Avoid the Clash of Civilizations* (London: Continuum, 2003).

Sage, Lorna, *Bad Blood: A Memoir* (London: Fourth Estate, 2000).

Sampson, Anthony, *Macmillan: A Study in Ambiguity* (London: Penguin, 1967).

Seldon, Anthony, *Major: A Political Life* (London: Weidenfeld & Nicolson, 1997).

Taylor, Charles, *A Secular Age* (London: Belknap, 2007).

Temple, William, *Christianity and Social Order* (London: Shepeard-Walwyn/SPCK, 1976).

Tönnies, Ferdinand (ed./tr. Charles P. Loomis), *Community and Society* (New York: Harper & Row, 1963).

Waines, David, *An Introduction to Islam* (Cambridge: CUP, 1995).

Woodhead, Linda and Heelas, Paul (eds), *Religion in Modern Times: An Interpretive Anthology* (Oxford: Blackwell, 2000).

Wright, Andrew, *Critical Religious Education, Multiculturalism and the Pursuit of Truth* (Cardiff: University of Wales Press, 2007).

Young, Michael, *Family and Kinship in East London* (London: Routledge & Kegan Paul, 1957).

Zebiri, Kate, *British Muslim Converts: Choosing Alternative Lives* (London: Oneworld, 2008).

Index

Index